How to Deal with Difficult People

Andrew Costello, C.SS.R.

LIGUORI
PUBLICATIONS

One Liguori Drive
Liguori, Missouri 63057
(314) 464-2500

Imprimi Potest:
Edmund T. Langton, C.SS.R.
Provincial, St. Louis Province
The Redemptorists

Imprimatur:
+ John N. Wurm, S.T.D., Ph.D.
Vicar General, Archdiocese of St. Louis

ISBN 0-89243-128-8
Library of Congress Catalog Card Number: 80-81751
Copyright © 1980, Liguori Publications

Printed in U.S.A.

Cover Design by Jim Corbett

*To Jean
who
taught a lot of us how
to understand each other*

TABLE OF CONTENTS

INTRODUCTION

Many are skilled in talking *about* difficult people, but few are skilled in talking *with* difficult people.

This book deals with the difficult people in our lives — those we can't stand or understand, those we can't stomach, those who cause us real pain.

It contains ideas gleaned from conversations with friends and readings from books. But mainly these thoughts come from watching people — including myself — dealing with difficult people.

Here are some of the ways people react to the problems we face in this area. They: *avoid them . . . . . divorce them . . . . . love them . . . . . hate them . . . . pray for them . . . . . get drunk . . . . . yawn . . . . talk to them . . . . . talk about them . . . leave a book like this around, hoping that the difficult person will pick it up and read it.*

Obviously, some of the above methods destroy human relationships. These pages have been written from a constructive viewpoint. This book uses common sense, sharpened by modern psychology, to integrate into a Christian view our relationships with other people.

Since grace builds on nature — God comes to us as we are — the questions asked and answered here begin with ourselves and the means provided by common sense in our dealings with difficult people. With this deeper, more defined self-knowledge, we then go on to the part that God must play in this area of our lives.

The questions asked and answered in this book are the following: Who are the difficult people in our lives, and why do we find them so? Are we willing to seek a better way to handle them? Do we have the courage to make a definite decision on this point? *(Chapter One)* Is it better to face them or avoid them? *(Chapter Two)* Should we consult a third party? *(Chapter Three)* Are our expectations about them reasonable or unreasonable? *(Chapter Four)* Is the problem a result of our seeing things differently? *(Chapter Five)* Is the problem a matter of different personality types? *(Chapter Six)* Are we allowing God to enter the picture? *(Chapter Seven)* Do we really believe that people can change? *(Chapter Eight)* Do we know how to dialogue? *(Chapter Nine)* Is there a way to integrate our natural methods with God's supernatural ways of dealing with difficult people? *(Chapter Ten)*

1
AWARENESS AND DECISION

We all want to know *HOW TO* deal with the difficult people in our lives. But to do so demands a certain discipline on our part. We have to go through a learning experience which makes us become *aware* of where we stand at the moment, and we have to *decide* what we are going to do about it.

Built upon these two steps — awareness and decision — this book points out the problems and primes the reader for solutions. A wife, for example, may discover that she is raiding the refrigerator or haunting the liquor cabinet because her husband comes home late almost every night. If she really wants to stop overeating or over-drinking, she must make up her mind to deal with the problem of her "late" husband. But she herself must make the decision. Books cannot make it for her.

Awareness means waking up. It shows us who we are and who we could be. It provides us with a dream, a vision. It says, for example, that we are fed up with the way we have been dealing with a certain person at work or with the direction our marriage has taken. And suddenly we say to ourselves, "There must be a better way of handling this."

This "better way" is possible because all personal relationships have a religious dimension. All of life has this deeper dimension below the surface. Relationships thus provide the potential for communion with God through friendship with others.

All problem relationships contain the seeds of their own solutions. Awareness to the situation can lead to a turnaround — a conversion resulting from reconciliation.

All improvement in personal relations — which entails insightful and deliberate effort to reconcile — have a *religious dimension,* even if the persons involved do not have an "up front" awareness of it. But we *can* have explicit awareness of this side of relationship, if we so choose. By seeing it in religious terms, people *whose religious development has been healthy* can bring about improvement.

And every improvement in our dealings with a difficult person is not only a "social" improvement; it is also a deepening of our "spiritual" lives with God — and with others. To love one's neighbor out of love for God is to love God. To better our love for neighbor also has a positive influence on relationships with still other people in our lives. (This we can see for ourselves, if we pay attention.) So, the "psychological," the "social," and the "spiritual" sides of personal relationships are all related.

AWARENESS

To become aware in this area involves three things. Having determined the difficult people in our lives, we ask ourselves *why* they are difficult for us. We look to *how* we have dealt with them in the past and *how* we can improve the situation in the future.

Who Are They?

Most families have at least one difficult person: an alcoholic father or mother; an interfering mother-in-law or father-in-law; a teenager addicted to either drugs, anger, foul language, loud music, or self.

Most businesses have one: a boss who plays favorites or a fellow worker who plays around; a gossip; a person who, with one word, can make everyone else wish Monday morning were Friday afternoon; a worker who avoids responsibilities like the plague.

Most parishes have one: a know-it-all — let's call her Nancy — who takes over every meeting, ignoring the rights of others; a do-nothing person who refuses to help the community in any way.

Who are the three most difficult people in your life? Write their names down on a separate piece of paper. Now, leave space under each name for three reasons why you feel that they bother you.

Name: _____ *Name:* _____ *Name:* _____

1.   1.   1.
2.   2.   2.
3.   3.   3.

Why Are They Difficult?

Difficulties between people are often in the area of feelings, and feelings are hard to put into words.

We are relieved once we can pinpoint the causes of our problems. We need to know. We need to label them in some way.

The people living in Philadelphia during the days of "The Legionnaires' Disease" wanted to know the cause of this strange sickness. After much research, doctors finally found the cause. It was a disease somewhat like pneumonia. And the more that doctors found out about it, the more relaxed people became — especially in Philadelphia. We are helped in much the same way when we can identify the causes of our problems. Once these are known, it will be easier to find a cure.

Why do some people "bug" us? What are the causes of friction between us and others? What are the labels for interpersonal diseases?

The answers to such questions are many. We can speak in generalities and say "selfishness" is the basic cause of most problems. Or we can be quite specific and say that the problem started because of "a certain remark my sister-in-law made at a wedding in July of 1978." And this latter approach is much better.

A wife may feel her husband is one of the three most difficult people in her life because he makes her nervous, and he is selfish. But these causes are too general, too vague. After more research, she might give these three specific reasons. "First of all, he constantly makes uncouth noises; and this embarrasses me, especially when he does this in public. Secondly, at home, he just sits there and never talks to me anymore. He drinks his beer, goes out, comes back with his paper, reads it, turns on the TV and falls asleep till it's time to go to bed. Thirdly, he upsets me because he'll be retiring next year, and that means I'll have to put up with his bad manners both day and night." (These are definitely more specific reasons.)

Of course, we can think of other cases: a wife who has become a problem for her husband; a child who has problems with his or her parents; parents who have problems with their children. The list is endless.

Sin: A Notable Cause

As we probe for the reasons why in this area, we may get some help from psychiatrists. We all act and react in certain ways because of our early training and the mindsets we have developed through the years. But what we must not overlook is the mystery of sin. We know this down deep, but we often find it difficult to admit it to ourselves. Yet whenever there is conflict between people, there is sin. God's will, God's dream for his world is not being realized. Somebody is refusing to understand. Somebody is being selfish. Sin then is a basic cause of the difficulties and troubles between people. Sin is what fractures and ruptures relationships.

But some people refuse to admit this. For many, sin is not an "in" word today. It is too abstract, and maybe we would like to keep it that way. Perhaps in the past we labeled things as sin that really weren't. And now because of the discoveries of depth psychology about the behavior of human beings — why we do things — we tend to think that moral theology and religion are obsolete. For many, then, the word "sin" has lost its meaning.

But when we speak of specific sins, we soon realize that sin is very much alive and that it is a serious reality, as serious as cancer. For example:

Jealousy: A husband hates weddings and other festive occasions because his wife loves to dance, and he can't stand it. His roast beef gets cold as he sits there feeding on jealousy, watching his wife dancing with a friend of the family who is ten years younger than he is.

Non-forgiveness: Many major disagreements between a husband and a wife are caused by one or the other bringing up a mistake made six, eight, ten years before.

Drugs: A teenage son or daughter forms a drug habit and drops out of college. The result is unbearable family tension and thousands of education dollars wasted.

Lies: A series of lies and broken promises between a couple with three children leads eventually to divorce. The result is five damaged people, bad memories, money problems, and extreme fear about the future.

Neglect: A 70-year-old widow suffers from anxiety and loneliness because only one of her seven children calls or visits her. (Most of the children live within 50 miles of her nursing home.)

We see, then, that sin *is* as real and as deadly as cancer. If we take the time out to dig deeper into the *cause* of our problems, we'll have to admit that sin is the root cause of our troubles.

Our religious traditions keep telling us this; but sin seems to harden our hearts, and the result is spiritual blindness and deafness.

Ezekiel, the prophet, described sin as a rust that forms and then ruins the metal of our lives (Ez 24:1-14). We worry when rust ruins our cars, but we seem unconcerned about the rust of sin eating away at our relationships.

Saint Paul, in writing to the people of Galatia, gave a long list of specific sins that were causing problems between the people residing there. He was giving answers to the WHY question. He urged them to be *aware* of and avoid: "lewd conduct, impurity, licentiousness, idolatry, sorcery, hostilities, bickering, jealousy, outbursts of rage, selfish rivalries, dissensions, factions, envy, drunkenness, orgies, and the like" (Gal 5:19-21).

(Now, using that same sheet of paper with your problem people on it, write down three specific reasons why you find these three people difficult.)

How Do You Deal with Them?

How to deal with difficult people is easier to answer than the *why* question. We can only surmise why people act the way they do. As the familiar Indian saying goes, we have never "walked in their moccasins for twelve moons," nor have they walked in ours.

We answer the question "How?" by looking at our own behavior. We can see actions. We can hear ourselves counting to ten or twenty instead of screaming at a fellow worker who drives us crazy.

But that doesn't mean that solutions to problems are easy. How do parents deal with a 25-year-old son who refuses to work, will not leave home, and will not stop drinking? How does a husband/wife deal with a wife/husband who refuses to talk about a problem marriage?

How do *you* cope with those difficult people who infuriate you? If you are running in the human race, you are already doing something to deal with them. But *what* are you doing? What are your patterns?

To clarify this for yourself, once again write on a separate sheet the names of your three most difficult persons. Now write below each name three specific ways you deal with them.

Name: _____ *Name:* _____ *Name:* _____
1.   1.   1.
2.   2.   2.
3.   3.   3.

Remember that know-it-all (we called her Nancy on page 11) who drives you crazy at every parish meeting? You put her name at the top of one of your columns. How are you dealing with her right now? Perhaps you write down something like this: "I talk about her at the coffee break and over the phone the following day. I keep telling others that we have to figure out a way to get her off the parish council. I try to prevent her from talking too much by looking at my watch, by shuffling papers, by moving my chair as soon as she begins to speak." (Next, you follow the same procedure for the other two names on the list.)

Now you are fully *aware* of how you deal with these people. So you ask yourself whether you really want to continue acting this way. You must make a *decision* about your behavior.

DECISION

Very simply put, decision means making a resolution to change. We actually start moving in the direction we have taken. And how we act for at least a month after that tells us whether or not we really made a decision at all.

Awareness has led us to this position, but we know that we will need help of some kind to persevere in our decision.

How Prayer Helps

Some people turn to God. Parents, for example, pray to God for help in dealing with a problem child. They ask God for patience — with that neighbor's son who comes zooming in on his motorcycle at 1:30 almost every morning. They go to church for years, praying for their children who have stopped going to church.

Do prayers work? Can prayer change people?

Yes, if we concentrate more on ourselves than others.

Perhaps one reason why some of our prayers are unanswered is because we forget the other side of prayer: our side. The old proverbs point this out: "Pray, but row to shore." "Pray for potatoes, but pick up a hoe."

Prayer works if it gives us the grace to get up off

our knees and do something constructive about a problem. It can lead us to reach out for marriage counseling even if our partner refuses to go. It can lead to Al-Anon, the Alcoholic Anonymous group for relatives and friends of alcoholics. It can instill the courage to speak peacefully to the parents of that boy whose motorcycle disturbs our sleep so much.

Prayer works if it leads us to deeper compassion, forgiveness, and understanding of the difficult person.

Prayer works if it teaches us to keep searching to do the Father's will.

Prayer works if it gets us to start with ourselves — to search into our attitudes, our own sinfulness.

Prayer works if it causes us to ask ourselves, "How responsible are we for this problem?"

Prayer works if it reminds us to confess that we have used sinful and immature ways of dealing with the difficult people in our lives — like talking destructively behind their backs.

Prayer works if it makes us realize that dealing with difficult people is a problem with no easy solutions, and that self-help books alone — not even the Bible — will solve the problem. We personally must use the grace of God obtained through prayer to solve our problems with difficult people.

We need to make a statement at least to ourselves on how we will try to improve our relationships with the people around us, especially the difficult ones. We need to know ourselves better, becoming aware of our mindsets. Then we can make a *decision* to go forward with God at our side.

SUMMARY

This chapter has explained the meaning of *awareness* and *decision*, especially as they apply to the difficult people in our lives. We know who they are, why they bother us, and how we have treated them in the past. We have decided that there is a better way to deal with them, and now we are ready to find that way.

2
FLIGHT OR FIGHT?

Once we have decided to deal with the difficult people in our lives, we have a choice between flight or fight.

What is our established pattern? Do we avoid difficult people like the plague, or do we go right up to them and say, "We have a problem here that needs to be straightened out"?

FLIGHT

Flight, escape, avoidance is the usual way people deal with difficult people. We see on which side of the street they intend to walk, and we walk the opposite side. We watch where they sit, and we find a chair as far away as possible. We take the backstairs because they always take the frontstairs.

At times, avoidance is the best procedure. It takes a great amount of emotional energy to be always asserting, confronting, as we face difficult people. We may slip and make a damaging mistake. We may be misquoted and thus destroy an already shaky relationship. We may acquire the reputation of being as abrasive as sandpaper.

But flight or avoidance can also be dangerous and destructive, especially when the situation *demands* interaction or confrontation. Excessive drinking has destroyed many a family because nobody said anything to the drinker. As Robert

Louis Stevenson wrote, "The cruelest lies are often told in silence."

Bad Effects

The destructive side of flight is usually wrapped in silence. Often, by keeping silent, running away, escaping, we destroy not only the difficult person but ourselves as well.

Flight is movement. It takes energy. Those who are constantly on the run are always tired. Holding something in can do real damage to the walls of the stomach. Worrying about a problem with another can cause negligence of work.

Many a marriage has been destroyed because of a "silent" partner. People marry because it is not good to be alone (Gn 2:18). But marriage that deteriorates into silent, lonely lonesomeness is killing, as the following poem indicates:

> Silence,
> Silent silence,
> Cold arctic silence,
> So quiet,
> So powerful,
> Sitting there
> Like a loaded gun,
> Pointed at my head,
> Pointed at my heart,
> When we are angry
> And have to drive home alone,
> Together in the silence.

People think the divorce rate is getting high. The silent unofficial divorce rate is even higher.

A wife stays downstairs every night, watching Johnny Carson on TV. When she knows her husband is surely asleep, she climbs the stairs, relieved that one more day is over without having to deal with him.

A husband leaves the house night after night. His excuses: bowling, the Right to Life Movement, the Knights of Columbus, the local bar, a parish meeting. For twenty years, he's been living an "unofficial divorce," perhaps without even being aware of it.

Such couples might even get upset when they hear that one of their married children is getting a legal divorce. But mom and dad should not be too surprised. For years, the children have seen their parents resorting to newspapers, television — anything and everything — as an excuse for not communicating. And when their parents did talk, it was usually about work, the weather, the neighbors, always avoiding the real issue — their relationship.

Teenagers too contribute to the problem. When parents become "difficult" and start clamping down on them because of poor schoolwork, a messy room, annoying friends, they soon become magicians: They disappear in a flash. A father screams at his 15-year-old son or daughter, "Where have you been lately? We never see you around here anymore. Your mother kills herself to prepare a Sunday dinner for you and the family, and where are you?" And the only response is a loud silence.

But inside these silent persons, angry thoughts are churning. These unspoken words can become poison flowing through the system, causing headaches and ulcers. They can become inner walls built to hide silent persons from the problem people they should be facing.

"People need people." A teddy bear, a dog, a cat, a bottle of scotch, television — these are all poor substitutes for people. The teenage girl, who locks herself in her room and clamps on her stereo headset so she can't hear even loud knocking on her door, is losing out on the benefits of family — unless they too are into the same flight pattern. If a plant is not cared for, it dies. As the family goes, so go the individual members.

From this negative side then, outright flight or silent retreat can destroy both self and the people around us. It can lead to various kinds of escape: overeating, overworking, overdrinking. It can stunt growth and development, moving people deeper and deeper into themselves.

Good Effects

But flight can also be constructive. If we responded with a fight every time somebody bothered us, we would need many more hospitals and cemeteries.

Seneca, a first-century Roman statesman, writer, and philosopher, said, "The greatest remedy for anger is delay." When we are angry, the old practice of counting to ten before we speak is still a wise procedure. We all need time to assess the situation. We need time to retreat. We need time to build up strength in order not to react in a destructive way.

Where words would fail, silence often delivers the message. For example, a mother grew tired of yelling at her teenage son for his sloppy room. So, she just sat back and let the dirty clothes pile up. She simply avoided that room. Eventually, her son came out of his "cave" waving a dirty white rag. "Okay, Mom, I surrender. You win. What's the problem?" And, instead of screaming back, "I'll tell you what the problem is," she sat down at the peace table with him, and they talked about a lot of problems. As a result, the son learned what it meant to be a part of a community (a family). He began to share the responsibilities in the upkeep of the house.

Flight, escape, silence, avoidance — these *can* be practical ways of saying something to others. The silence will make them aware that something is wrong. This kind of passive aggression will work if it makes people recognize that a problem does exist.

So, flight can have either good or bad effects. Our task is to choose the one best suited for the situation at hand.

FIGHT

Some people speak up and let difficult people know exactly how they feel. They fight back. Because "fight" has hostile overtones, perhaps it is not the best word to use here. "Assertiveness" might better describe what is meant. In any case, fight is the opposite of flight. Instead of holding back and keeping silent in the presence of a difficult person, we speak up and let him or her know exactly where we stand.

At times, fight courts disaster, but it can make difficult people finally realize how we react to their behavior.

Unhealthy Results

Obviously, fighting is useless when its end result is destruction of self or the other party. It is extremely harmful when we lose control of ourselves, saying and doing things we did not intend to say or do. Sometimes it is destructive because it takes place at the wrong time and in the wrong place. And only God knows how much damage is done when it hurts the innocent, especially little children.

There are times when and places where we feel like fighting back. But so often our jobs, our livelihoods, our families' security demand "keeping our cool," and we have to "bite our tongues."

In one of his writings, Anton Chekhov, the Russian author, has one of his characters say: "People must never be humiliated." This should be uppermost in our minds when we enter the "fight" arena. If we fight only to humiliate, then it is time to reassess our values: What are we doing, and why are we doing it?

We may come home from a meeting feeling bad because, while arguing with someone, we lost control of ourselves. Now we get angry because we got angry. We can't sleep. We toss and turn. We keep thinking of what we should have said or should not have said.

Yes, fighting can be unhealthy, harmful, and destructive — not only for the challenged but also for the challenger.

Healthy Results

But fighting can also be constructive. It can be a healthy means of communication, telling people who we are and where we stand. Marriages, families, groups, churches, if they are to function well, need an atmosphere of openness where all persons can assert both their agreements and disagreements. Better in public than in private; otherwise, we tend to tear each other apart over the telephone and at the coffee break — but with a third party.

But we need to learn the techniques of a "fair fight." Virginia Satir, a family therapist, tells couples, "Everyone needs a way of fighting." A wife, for example, may choose the assertive method; her husband may prefer to sit down and talk quietly about the situation.

This couple could very well learn from the cartoon which shows a wife talking to her husband. The caption reads, "Would you please stop being so understanding, and argue with me?"

In recent years, much emphasis has been placed on learning how to assert oneself. Judging from the number of books, courses, and workshops on this topic, there must be many people who feel a need for this — which could mean that many people have been avoiders in the past.

Still, a great number of people seem to prefer *flight to fight* when dealing with difficult people. When we speak out for something, we run the risk of being called "pushy" people or troublemakers. Morever, if we stand up for something and our judgment in the matter turns out wrong, we leave ourselves in an exposed position. The other person now has ammunition that can last from here to eternity. Those who sit back and say nothing about the point at issue can enjoy never having said the wrong thing.

When we waver between *flight* or *fight,* we should follow our "gut" feelings. We can run away from others, but we can't run away from ourselves. If we never learn to assert our thoughts and feelings, we may appear tranquil on the outside, but we are tormented from within. Those who let off steam may make mistakes, but they are probably healthier than those who don't.

• Are you *aware* of your pattern?
• Are you a teapot or a pressure cooker?

Being assertive does not mean pouring boiling-hot water on a difficult person — even though we are steaming. When done properly, it becomes top-level communication. Whether it should take place face-to-face at a public meeting or in private conversation depends upon the circumstances.

How to Be Assertive

Tom is a member of his parish council. He seldom, if ever, says a word of disagreement at their meetings; but later he voices his disapproval to others. John, the parish council president, telephones Tom and diplomatically asks him about this, but Tom denies that he has said anything. At the next meeting, in front of everyone, John says calmly, "Tom, I heard that you disapproved of our recent decision about the microphone system for the church. Could you tell us here and now whether you disagree with getting a new system or not? I personally think that a parish council needs to air differences openly; each member should express his or her opinion in the presence of the whole group." Silence and tension fill the room. Tom will now have to react. This should be a learning experience for him. Perhaps he will suffer enough to realize that he is responsible as a parish council member to speak up at the meetings.

However, we should not be too quick to condemn Tom. There may be more to the story than meets the eye. It could be that the other members of the parish council constantly attack him behind his back. Or maybe John, the parish council president, does not allow for any disagreements because he does only what the pastor tells him to do.

Being assertive exposes us to many risks. Once we "correct" someone, we have to be ready to be corrected in return by the other person. Once John brings something up to Tom at the meeting, then John has to be ready to have things brought up to him.

When to Be Assertive

There are times when we must speak up. If an obvious injustice is being committed, we have a duty to intervene. We cannot sit back and allow difficult persons to destroy others and themselves. Active confrontation becomes a "must" in situations like the following.

The mayor of a certain small town had been drinking too much for years. He was a brilliant man; and, although the members of his council were more than competent, he practically ran the town single-handedly. But as his drinking became heavier, his thinking became lighter. The whole town was going to pot. Everybody seemed to know his problem, except himself. He bumbled through meetings. He staggered through the streets, thinking he was God's gift to the world. Nobody said anything. He could not see what everybody saw — that he was slowly killing himself.

A new member was elected to the council. He watched. He listened. He heard the other members talking about their alcoholic mayor. He overheard the townspeople saying, "Somebody ought to do something."

The new member finally went to the mayor and simply said, "Hey, you're killing yourself with booze. You're drinking too much. Everybody in town knows it. You may think that you are God's gift to the world — and you are when you're sober — but right now you're not. You're a bum! You need help, and I'll help you get it."

It worked. It was excellent shock therapy. Breaking down the mayor's defenses, it woke him up enough to ask for help. He got it. Today he's quite active in Alcoholics Anonymous. He's using the outstanding gifts God gave him to help others.

Of course, active confrontation doesn't always work that smoothly. Sometimes, people with drinking problems never hear a word we say. Our assertive words and actions may only make a dent in the other person's armor; but that dent will be remembered when the person makes his or her own decision to do something about the problem. (This will be discussed in later chapters.)

• Which pattern do you usually follow — flight or fight?

- If you choose "flight," is it because you lack courage, or because common sense dictates it in this instance?
- If you choose "fight," do you make a special effort to control your emotions?
- Have you ever tried to balance off the bad points of your problem people with their good points?

SUMMARY

This chapter has discussed two different ways of dealing with difficult people. We can run, or we can stay and fight. Some people find one pattern easier than the other. Both choices have their good and bad qualities. But we ourselves must decide on the best course of action according to the circumstances.

3
SEEKING HELP

Knowing that there is "a time to speak" and "a time to remain silent" does help us in our personal relationships with others. But how can we be certain which is the better method to follow? Obviously, we need further help.

Most people try to solve this dilemma by taking their problem to a third party. They look for someone in whom they can confide. Theirs is an honest attempt to sort out the reasons why they find this certain person so difficult.

Our purpose in seeking out a third party should be the same. We have thought over the situation ourselves; but, most of us will have to admit that our personal opinions may be prejudiced. So, it is always smart to get an unbiased opinion from a third party.

But who are these people and how do we find them?

FINDING COUNSELORS

If our problem is very serious, we might need professional help from a psychiatrist, a psychologist, a marriage counselor. We can find them in the yellow pages, of course. But our family doctor or local pastor should be able to recommend one to us.

But what if we're not sure just how serious the problem is? What if we feel we're not ready for professional help? What about the ordinary everyday problems we all have with people we find difficult to take? Is there anybody who can help us in these areas?

Well, every neighborhood has someone who is just the person we need. He or she may be an old friend, a neighbor, a nun, a priest, a doctor — people from all walks of life.

We may call them "counselors" if we wish. But they don't go by that name. They are: Tom, Dick, Harry, Mary, Jane, and Maureen. More important than their titles are the skills they possess. Who, then, among our acquaintances make excellent "counselors"? The following pages will describe the type of people we are seeking.

Good Listeners

The first quality of a good counselor is the ability to listen. If we approach someone with a problem and he or she begins immediately to monopolize the conversation, then we know we have knocked on the wrong door. If the brief statement of our problem triggers countless stories from our "listener," then we don't want that person for a counselor. Ambrose Bierce, an American writer of the 19th century, defines a bore as "a person who talks when we wish him to listen." We want ears more than a mouth.

But listening is not just silence. It is hard work. Good listeners block out their own lives and project themselves into the life of the other person. They empathize with that person's feelings and pains. They watch the other's eyes and hands. They try to understand what the other is really trying to understand for himself or herself.

Dr. Ralph G. Nichols, a specialist in communications, tells us that people speak at a speed of approximately 125 words per minute, but we think at a speed of 500 words per minute. Most of us use this time wondering about other things — "What's for supper?" or "What's on TV tonight?" But good listeners use this time trying to figure out what the other person is saying or not saying, what he or she is feeling, what pains are being experienced at the moment.

All of us find it hard to concentrate. It takes discipline to do so. Good listeners have acquired this habit. They brush other thoughts aside and pinpoint their attention on the problem being presented.

Good listeners are hard to find. But if we open up our own ears and listen, if we open up our own eyes and see, we'll find them. During a conversation, they are the ones who ask brief questions about what the other person has just said. They are sincerely interested in others and their lives. At times they may sum up the other person's words: "What you seem to be saying is . . . ." Yet it won't sound forced or phony.

Most of us are deaf. We are so wrapped up in ourselves. Because of this, we don't notice the few good listeners who are in our midst.

• Who is the best listener you ever met?
• When you would like to discuss a problem, to whom do you go?
• Has anyone ever come to you with a problem?
• Did you listen?
• Did that person ever come back to you?

• Did you ever check to see how things worked out?

Objective Thinkers

Good counselors think objectively. They do not take sides. If, for example, our complaint is about a son or a daughter who refuses to go to church, we should not expect to be "stroked" (see page 59). Their sole concern is to give a fair judgment.

If, after listening to our story, they have some "bad news" for us, they will not hesitate to deliver it. They know there are no "magic" solutions to problems. And if we indicate by our attitudes that we are looking for the complete answer to all our problems, they will not hesitate to tell us that this is an unreasonable expectation.

Objective thinkers make good counselors because they have the ability to bypass their own subjective relationships. Perhaps our story will remind them of their story: they may also have children who stopped going to church. But they leave these subjective feelings aside and apply themselves seriously to our problem.

G. K. Chesterton said of St. Francis of Assisi: "There never was a man who looked into those brown, burning eyes without being certain that Francis was really interested in him . . . that he, himself, was being valued and taken seriously."

That's the kind of person we're all looking for — someone who will examine our problem objectively because he/she is not afraid to look us in the eye. Only after such an experience will we be able to take ourselves seriously. And until we take ourselves seriously, we won't be able to take others seriously.

Experienced People

Good counselors have been through the mill, as we say. They have experienced the pains of life and the growth that comes with pain. They can laugh because they have learned how to heal their own lives. In his book *The Wounded Healer,* Father Henri Nouwen reminds us that such people can offer their own experience "as a source of healing to those who are often lost in the darkness of their own misunderstood sufferings" (page 89).

These experienced people are not really hard to find. We all must have heard at one time or another, "Go talk to Father *So-and-so,* he'll understand. He's been through it all." Many others before us have had to face the question of whether or not to put a parent in a nursing home when he or she started to become "very difficult." There are any number of older people who have had problems raising their children, and are willing to share the knowledge they gained from the experience. And countless are those who have faced sickness and death in the family. Of course, they have no degrees from all these life courses, but their experience certainly qualifies them as excellent counselors.

Our senior citizens may not be able to jog and run up and down stairs, but many of them would enjoy talking to us and delighting us with their wisdom. There are many retired priests who have been placed "on the shelf," but they would make great counselors. They would be more than happy to take on "second careers" as spiritual directors for all those people who are starving for someone to listen to them and get a clearer direction for their lives.

"Wisdom comes from suffering and age." Old people are not "out of touch, sexless, and inflexible." People who have experienced forty and fifty years of dealing with difficult people can make good counselors.

But, here is a word of caution. There are many people who have experienced life to the full, but they have never really learned from their experience. They do not make good counselors. The saying is true: "There's a world of difference between having twenty years' experience and having one year's experience twenty times." Some people just cruise along, letting life happen to them, leaving the driving to someone else; other people take the wheel in hand, directing the flow of their lives, using their present experiences to guide their future lives. Some people learn; some people never learn.

Take the example of people who get married to the same problem three times in a row. The husband or wife may be different, but the problem remains the same. It seems they never learn from their mistakes. Could it be because they never reflect upon their experiences? The dynamic of AWARENESS and DECISION doesn't seem to be part of their lives. Wise and experienced people make good counselors. They can help us.

Challenging Persons

Good counselors challenge us to reflect on what is happening in our lives. They ask questions. Good questions start us thinking. And the right question — answered honestly — can change our lives.

Here are some questions often asked. "Does anybody else find this person difficult?" If you are the only one who does, then maybe you need some soul-searching. Perhaps you're just a busybody. "Who has the problem here? You or the other person? Is it more than a mannerism that is bothering you? Is it just a question of style? Is it jealousy?" Maybe the other person is upstaging you, and the problem lies with you — because you demand to be the center of attention. "Does this happen all the time or only when so-and-so is around?"

Other questions asked by a good counselor will help you put into words some of the thoughts you never before expressed. "Who says you have to solve all the problems you have with other people?" Maybe life consists of a series of personnel problems. "Are you trying to make people fit into a preconceived mold of your own design?" Our greatest sin, according to a sage of the age, is our inability to forgive others their otherness.

Here are some other questions a good counselor will ask. Answer them for yourself.

- Are you expecting too much of this person?
- Are you making sufficient allowance for human limitations?
- Are you presuming motives for his/her behavior — motives that for all you know may not be true at all?
- Are you afraid that this person may take away your job?

- As a parent, are you worrying about the "empty nest" left by your departing children?
- What is really going on in this problem you have with so-and-so, and why do you let it bother you?

The counselor's questions will vary according to circumstances. But one who is wise and experienced and who listens objectively will use them judiciously. They will help you to understand both yourself and the other person. They will get you in touch with the deeper layers of your own person, especially in the area of feelings.

. Counselors who do not ask questions are questionable.

Trustworthy Friends

Good counselors are true friends worthy of our trust. We feel safe with them, knowing that they will never reveal our secrets. They will respect our feelings and never betray our confidences.

Such people have all the qualities of true friendship expressed in the following words:

> Friendship is the comfort,
> the inexpressible comfort,
> of feeling safe with a person,
> having neither to weigh thoughts
>   nor measure words,
> but pouring all right out
>   just as they are —
> chaff and grain together —
> certain that a faithful, friendly hand
> will take and sift them,
> keep what is worth keeping
> and with a breath of comfort,
> blow the rest away.

These are inspiring words on the beauty of friendship. But there is nothing more beautiful than to see them take flesh in the behavior of someone who has earned the right to be called our "friend."

We leave such a friendly counselor, feeling free. The knots in our nerves have been loosened, even untied. We walk away knowing that we have confided in someone who was not shocked by our "weird" feelings about a brother or a sister. Our friend has challenged us to make the right decision on our own; and we depart knowing that we may return if further help is needed.

SUMMARY

To help us decide whether to run away from our problems or to stand up and fight back, we often need the help of a third party. If we need professional help, we visit a psychiatrist, a psychologist, a marriage counselor.

But in most cases, we can turn to special friends — those who will listen to us and make objective judgments, those who, in their wisdom and experience, are unafraid to challenge us, and those with whom we can trust our secrets.

4
WHAT DO WE EXPECT?

At the heart of every difficulty we have with others is the problem of expectations. We feel that our problem people should act differently. "Why can't they change?" "Why can't they be the way we expect them to be?" "Why don't they live up to our expectations?"

As we saw in the last chapter, a good counselor will help us to realize that "people problems" are the main problems everyone faces. If we ask any manager, bishop, bus driver, usher, teacher, they will all tell us that "thing problems" are easy; it's "people problems" that disturb them and take up most of their energy.

When we reveal our problem to a counselor, what we are actually saying is the following: "This other person (Nancy, Tom, our son-in-law, our husband/wife) is not living up to our expectations. We are expecting a rose garden, but maybe they never promised us one."

College students expect the final exams to deal only with questions that were stressed in class. Husbands expect their wives to have the same sexual outlook as they do. Parents expect their children to marry persons only after their final approval. Grandparents expect their children and their children's children to drop in at least once a month, or at least to give them a call. Idealists expect other people to live up to their idealistic principles, and complain when people don't.

Problems in this area can arise in various ways:

a. When our expectations are not met.
b. When we try to force people to meet our expectations.
c. When we begin to believe it's our fault that other people are not living up to our expectations.
d. When we start to think that certain other people don't like or love us when they fail to live up to our expectations.
e. When we are not *aware* of our own or others' expectations.

Every person then is a box of expectations. As we have already seen, we need someone, a good friend, a counselor who will get us to open up that box and pour the contents out on the table. We need to become *aware* of our own expectations.

REASONABLE AND UNREASONABLE EXPECTATIONS

Some of our expectations are *reasonable* and some are *unreasonable*. This is basic common sense, but often it is not understood. So we continue to be frustrated with wives, husbands, children, teachers, leaders, because they are not living up to the expectations we set up for them to meet. What's worse, we never tell them.

To help us sort out our thinking in this area, here is a list of questions to answer. A simple R (for reasonable) or U (for unreasonable) will do.

• Is it reasonable or unreasonable for Catholic parents to think it's their fault that a son got divorced and is now getting remarried to a divorced woman?

- Is it reasonable or unreasonable to expect people never to have bad days?
- Is it reasonable or unreasonable to presume that people will make mistakes while driving, have accidents, and even cause deaths?
- Is it reasonable or unreasonable to expect husbands and wives to change and develop new ideas, dream new dreams, and set new values after they are married?
- Is it reasonable or unreasonable for a mother to expect her son and daughter-in-law to drop over with the children every Sunday afternoon?
- Is it reasonable or unreasonable for parents to think it's their fault that their children no longer attend church services?
- Is it reasonable or unreasonable to expect a 67-year-old priest to celebrate Mass like a 27-year-old priest?

Most of the above questions can be answered without any difficulty. But despite this, some of our own answers will differ from those of others. We all have different expectations; and various circumstances in our personal lives will color what we think is reasonable or unreasonable. This is why it is so important to talk over our problems and expectations with a close friend. He or she will help us discover what is best for all concerned.

Let's look now at three areas of our lives where expectations — reasonable and unreasonable — play such an important part.

In Marriage Relationships

On their wedding day brides and grooms say, "I do" with many and varied expectations in mind. If they reach their 25th Wedding Anniversary, they may repeat their vows in a solemn ceremony. What has happened to their young dreams and expectations? Some of them have been realized, some not. It is hoped that through the years their expectations have become more realistic, and that they themselves and their dreams are now being fulfilled.

Twenty-five years of living together ought to make a difference. Each day should make a difference. Marshall McLuhan once said that marriage, like any other relationship "must be remade by the contracting parties every day. It's a terrible illusion in many people's lives that if they don't match each other exactly, they ought to break up. They don't seem to consider the possibility of *making* as an alternative to *matching*."

William James, an American psychologist and philosopher, wrote: "Whenever two people meet, there are really six people present. There is each man as he sees himself, each man as the other person sees him, and each man as he really is." This same idea is also true of marriage. Soon after the wedding day, both partners begin to discover:

He is different than she thought he was.

She is different than he thought she was.

He is different than he thought he was.

She is different than she thought she was.

Movements like Marriage Encounter encourage couples to discuss this point with each other. Did Joe fall in love with the real person of Jane or only with the mask she presented before marriage? Did Jane fall in love with the real Joe? It is an *unreasonable expectation* for couples to enter marriage thinking that they have fully discovered their real identities. That's why both partners need a good sense of adventure and a good sense of humor. They also need the good sense to communicate with each other — especially concerning their expectations in the major areas of marriage: money, sex, and in-laws. Married couples should, therefore, arrange for sufficient time on a regular basis to clarify all the expectations they have of each other.

Unfortunately, however, many married people spend frustrating years fuming inwardly, talking to themselves and not talking to their partners about their lives together. Their bodies may be friends, but their emotions are total strangers.

Divorce spells out the ultimate announcement that two people have not met each other's expectations. It could also mean that they have given up trying to clarify or renegotiate their expectations of each other. In any case, boredom has set in. The dream they had on their wedding day has become a nightmare. They want out.

In Family Relationships

Often, the most difficult people in children's lives are their parents. Often, too, the most difficult people in parents' lives are their children.

Much is expected from people who live in community. When these people are family, expectations increase a thousandfold. So children have huge expectations of their parents, and parents have huge expectations of their children.

Some are reasonable expectations; some are unreasonable. If ever there is a need for reflecting, talking things over with each other, and discussing problems with a counselor, it is here in this area of relationships between parents and children.

And the problems do not always cease when Junior goes off to college or gets married or leaves home. There are too many people in their fifties still trying to live up to the unreasonable expectations of their parents — sometimes long after their parents have died. And, on the other hand, there are people in their thirties making unreasonable demands of their parents. They expect parents to be permanent stand-by baby sitters or they constantly impose on their parents when, through their own stupidity, they are in a bind. "Good ole dad and mom will bail us out again." There are people in their fifties who still get angry with a parent who asks how things are going. They seem to think it unreasonable for parents to show that they still love them.

Perhaps we have met doctors, lawyers, nuns, teachers who are unhappy in their professions. They "chose" these careers because "mommy" or "daddy" expected them to do so. Their unhappiness stems from resentment of their parents and anger at themselves for not speaking out when they had the chance. Most of us, too, have met people who married a "second choice" because the first choice didn't come up to their parents' expectations. Countless novels, plays, movies, and afternoon TV stories are based on such unfortunate circumstances. And the same dramas are being acted out daily in the homes and hearts of numerous families. Sometimes there is an even more complicated "soap opera" taking place in a given home than on the television screen.

Expectations of parents and children cause many of life's difficulties. Each generation — like each country — wants to be free, to be liberated. Parents need to cut the umbilical cord and the apron strings. Children need to go to school, to camp, to college; they need to be exposed to all the traditional ways of learning so they can discover for themselves how to stand alone — away from mom and dad and home.

We all can learn much from a certain film recently produced for teenagers and parents. It is about a mama bear and her two baby bears. When she feels they are big enough to be on their own, she leads them to a big tree and makes them climb it. Then she starts to move away. Naturally, the cubs climb back down the tree to follow their mama. But mama bear turns and growls at them. They scramble back up the tree. Once more mama bear moves away. The cubs cling to the tree and watch her disappear into the woods. But she is only hiding. Both cubs wait a bit longer and then slowly climb down the tree to go in search of mama. But mama bear comes roaring out of the bushes and scares them up the tree once again. The same thing happens a third time. Then the film shows the mama bear walking away alone into the woods. Her two little ones are now on their own.

Teenagers are usually fascinated by this film. They know (perhaps they can't put it in words) that this story is their story.

The ancient Greek dramatists taught a corresponding lesson in their plays. When adolescent boys and girls in ancient times went to see a play like *Orestes,* they saw on the stage what was happening in their hearts and minds. They discovered through a play that we all have guilt feelings about wanting to leave home: that it's normal to want to be free, and that it's normal for parents to hold back.

Letting go and holding on — these are the problems parents and children must face. Behind the questions of curfew, drinking, drugs, school marks, allowance, use of the car, dating, college, marriage, visits from the children, and old age loneliness is this ever-present dilemma of *expectations.*

In Parish Relationships

Besides marriage and family relationships, another key area where this issue of expectations presents itself is the local parish.

People often expect a priest who is quite limited in his speaking ability to preach homilies he really cannot give. Mr. Michael Perfection sits there in church on a given Sunday, frustrating himself with this unreasonable expectation he has of Father Severity. The following Sunday he goes to a later Mass hoping the homilist will be a different priest. But who walks down the aisle? Yes, it's Father Severity again. So Mr. Perfection uses his head. The next Saturday, he has his young daughter call the rectory to ask which Mass Father Younger will be celebrating. He attends the 11:30 Mass with high expectations about Father Younger. Once more he hears a poor homily. Father Younger just didn't have it that day. This time Mr. Perfection is really angry,

47

because he knows Father Younger can preach well. He has bragged about him to the men at work. (But if Mr. Perfection really thought about it, he would remember that Father Younger preaches well only on those few Sundays following his return from his yearly retreat.)

Often at parish council meetings this problem of reasonable and unreasonable expectations presents difficulties. People expect the pastor to do this and say that. Above all, he is not allowed to talk about money. If he does that, four people will get mad. Others expect the meeting to end at 9:00 P.M. sharp, as agreed upon, and it's now 9:24. Three people sit there angry, because that nun over there is not wearing her veil. The president is angry at five people who aren't even there. Three of those five actually prepared the agenda and never even showed up or called. The rest are uptight because Nancy (remember her) won't shut up!

The whole parish council, perhaps the whole parish, should reserve a special time for talking over their expectations of each other. Some groups have tried this. They take a large piece of paper and tape it to the wall. On the top they put in bold letters words like, "PASTOR" or "USHERS" or "NUNS" or "PARISH COUNCIL MEMBERS." Each member of the group then declares what he or she expects of the above persons and their roles. After all have had their say, the entire group votes by placing an "R" (for reasonable) or a "U" (for unreasonable) after each expectation.

Would it be possible for every parish to do something like this? This may be an unreasonable expectation — because it demands a huge amount of trust. It would depend very much upon the people involved. If the parish council president or the pastor or a few of those present are extremely difficult people, they might kill the idea immediately. And if Sister No-veil is present, she might be crushed if people listed their expectations of "NUNS" as "always available" — only to hear someone say: "But that's unreasonable. She's never around here on weekends."

Some groups, however, have a high level of trust. They would be able to put names like, "Father Severity" or "Father Younger" or "Nancy" at the top of the list and be extremely fair in evaluating their expectations of each particular person. Many groups have not reached this stage of trust, but every group in a parish can at least start the ball rolling with: "Let's check out all our expectations on this issue or for this program to see whether they are reasonable or not."

SUMMARY

Becoming *aware* of this dynamic of expectations — reasonable or unreasonable — will help clarify many issues involved in marriage, family, and parish relationships. If we find ourselves using these terms in everyday speech, then we're beginning to work these ideas into our lives. If we find people starting to use them in response to us, then we know that communication is improving in our search for a better understanding of how to deal with difficult people.

5
ROLES PEOPLE PLAY

Here we will propose two specific ways to treat the problems surrounding our dealings with difficult people: the imitation of models and the use of transactional analysis.

In the last chapter, we saw that the reason why we have difficulties with certain people is because they are not living up to our expectations. When we examine our expectations more closely, we find that they are based on "models." We want someone to be a model child, a model wife, a model boss; and we determine what the model is supposed to look like. We want others to follow our plan, our image, our blueprint for them. When they don't, we are frustrated. We are playing God — wanting to create man and woman in our image and likeness.

IMITATION OF MODELS

Janet expects her husband to treat her just as her dad treated her mom. She marries with that model for marriage in mind. She stands there alone in the kitchen doing the supper dishes, frustrated because her husband Hank is in the living room watching TV. (She still pictures her dad saying to her mom, "Honey, you cooked the supper, so I'll wash the dishes. Why don't you go out in the living room and relax?" Both her parents were equal partners. Neither was boss.) Soon after they were married, Janet found out that

Hank had a different idea about marriage. He came from a different kind of home. Not only that, Hank was also an ex-Marine sergeant. His model on how a house should be run was based on his training as a Marine. His word was command. No discussions were allowed. Janet and the children knew this by heart: ''The problem with the world today is that nobody respects authority anymore.''

If husbands and wives could sit down and construct the model they have in mind for their marriage, many of their problems could be eliminated. But many couples — never having seen their parents sit down to talk out their problems — are not *aware* of this method. This is sad because by imitating this model of calmly talking over their problems, they could arrive at a mutual *decision* for the future.

This imitation of a model has been very successful in a certain New Jersey retreat house. A lady named Jean always talked about models to get across her ideas. She was in charge of a marvelous staff of women who cooked, served tables, and took care of the other jobs in the upkeep of the house. At meetings, Jean would say, ''We're a family. We're not a business. One hand washes the other. Let's all help one another.''

Business firms are run on time clocks. Each person has a specific job to do, and ordinarily his or her responsibility ends at closing time. But a family model should be different. In a real home, everyone is expected to pitch in and help with the dishes and the upkeep of the house. We don't have time clocks in our homes.

Jean's retreat house was like that. Some days were not as busy as others, and the workers were allowed to go home early. But on busy days, there was extra work to do. Those who finished their jobs first were expected to help the others who were not yet finished. It worked. Everybody who came to the retreat house noticed the family atmosphere. The place certainly had the personal touch. Jean matched her words with her work. As boss she didn't sit behind a desk and give orders (BUSINESS MODEL); no, one minute she was at the stove, the next minute at the dishwasher or out in the dining room passing out the dessert (FAMILY MODEL).

Jean was tragically killed when a tractor-trailer crashed into the back of the car she was driving. Her loss was a devastating blow to the retreat house and to all her family and so many friends. Yet her family model, her vision, still lives on. The people at the retreat house now ask, "How would Jean do this?" In other words, "We're a family, and we have to keep her spirit going to help each other keep going."

In the back of our minds then, we all have a collection of pictures or images or models of what a good job, boss, movie, doctor, or book is. We constantly compare them with the models we have of them in our minds.

But most of the time, we are unconscious of all this. We are not *aware* that this is the main reason why, for example, we find Hank or Nancy so difficult.

- What models are you imitating?
- What qualities do you look for in others?

- Are your expectations of others reasonable or unreasonable?

TRANSACTIONAL ANALYSIS

In recent years, a number of practical books have been written to help us understand the models we use and the expectations we have in our treatment of difficult people. They advocate what is called transactional analysis — TA. These books do not feature the religious dimension in our lives, but they do give us a better understanding of how we act and react as human beings. Grace (God's presence and guidance) builds on human nature. Jesus says that we must love difficult people because all men and women are created in God's image. We love them out of love for God. We should be grateful, then, for any natural help we receive in following God's command to love all people without exception.

TA is an attempt to simplify the discoveries of psychotherapy and psychoanalysis — to make them more helpful to the average person. It uses short simple words. It can provide some practical insights for those who want to improve their relationships with all people. Even as these pages do, TA books make us *aware* of our inner selves and urge us to *decide* on a course of action for the future.

Parent, Adult, Child

TA teaches that each person has three ego (inner) states (selves) which are separate and distinct sources of behavior: the Parent, the Adult, and the Child (P-A-C). Our Parent houses our values and tells us how we "should" and "ought to" behave in all situations. Our Adult acts as our computer, gathering and processing information. Our Child houses our feelings, our spontaneity, our creativity, our spunk, our rebellion. Well-balanced personalities present a happy mixture of Parent, Child, and Adult — with the Adult in control.

Transactions take place between people by word or some other means of communication. The one who initiates the proceedings gives the *stimulus*; the one who answers gives the *response*. When we *expect* people to respond from a certain ego state, and they do, this is called a *complementary transaction*. When they do not, this is called a *crossed transaction*. TA books picture these transactions on charts somewhat like the following:

COMPLEMENTARY TRANSACTION

Adult Stimulus with Adult Response

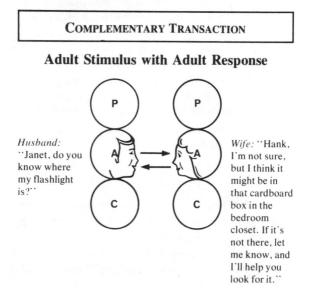

Husband: "Janet, do you know where my flashlight is?"

Wife: "Hank, I'm not sure, but I think it might be in that cardboard box in the bedroom closet. If it's not there, let me know, and I'll help you look for it."

A. Adult Stimulus
with Child-to-Parent Response

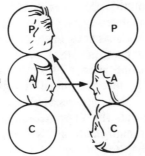

Husband:
"Janet, do you
know where
my flashlight
is?"

Wife: "Why
are you yelling
at me?"

B. Adult Stimulus
with Parent-to-Child Response

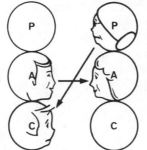

Husband:
"Janet, do you
know where
my flashlight
is?"

Wife: "You
never put
anything away.
Why do you
have to be so
careless all the
time?"

Of course, these are not the only kinds of
transactions, and there are variations of them all;
but these will serve as an introduction to the

system. (For further information, see the Reading List on page 127.)

Once we recognize the kind of transaction that has occurred, we analyze it (examine it thoroughly) to see what is happening between ourselves and the other person. Hence, the name "Transactional Analysis." This *awareness* will help us to *decide* what to do about the situation.

When we hear people coming at us as an authority, using words like: "should . . . do . . . don't . . . never . . . must . . . always . . . be good . . . ," they are probably speaking from their Parent state (P). They are acting like parents dealing with small children: "No, no, you mustn't do that," or "Stop it!" or "Say, 'Thank you.' " And sometimes their message isn't verbal at all; their gestures, the light in their eyes, the way they purse their lips says quite plainly: "Good boy!" or "Bad boy!" or "Grow up, will you!"

The Child state (C) is that of feelings, emotions, play, excitement, fears, smallness, and nail biting. It uses words and phrases like, "Let's have some fun . . . Gee whiz . . . Wow . . . Help! . . . I didn't do it . . . I'm no good." It's the state we're in when we're at the edge of our chair watching an exciting play, movie, or sporting event. It's the state the boss is in when he has a temper tantrum. It's the role the secretary plays when she makes a careless blunder and goes to the rest room to hide and perhaps cry.

The Adult state (A) is the one between the Parent and the Child. It is non-emotional, rational; it represents the reasoning side of a person. It uses words like, "Who . . . what . . . when . . . where . . . why . . . how?" An example: Suppose your boss calls you into his office, angry that you didn't finish a certain job. When the explosion is over, you calmly explain what happened and offer your opinions on how it can be corrected in the future. (The Parent in you would have warned: "Don't do this. It might cost you your job.")

Eric Berne and other TA specialists use two models — the tape recorder and the script — to help people further clarify what's happening inside themselves as they deal *(transact)* with other people. We can use these models when we are talking directly with other persons or just analyzing them in our own minds.

Tapes as Models

Doctor Wilder Penfield of the Montreal Neurological Institution, while doing brain surgery, stumbled upon the fact that if certain parts of the cortex of the brain were given electrical stimulation, the patient "re-lived" events that had happened in earlier life. He discovered that the memory is like a tape recorder. Berne and his associates then began to use this idea of the tape recorder as one of the models in their therapy sessions.

When we were small, we began to develop the Parent in us (P) by listening, recording, imitating, and mimicing our parents and other authority figures. Because our reasoning powers were undeveloped at the time, we accepted everything without question. If we were told that both Santa Claus and God had their big books for marking down when we were "naughty or nice," we believed it. This is how the traditions, values, beliefs, and "how-to's" are passed down from generation to generation — on our Parent tape. And these "sayings" (whether true or false) together with the attitude and example of our parents have all been recorded. They cannot be erased; but, as we shall see, they can be turned off.

At the same time — sort of like a stereo recorder — our Child tape was recording. It picked up all the joys and fears of childhood. If we had a happy childhood, it will stay with us for the rest of our lives. We'll know how to have fun. We'll know how to let our "hair down" and act like a child at a party. We won't sit there refusing to play some game saying, "I can't," or "This is stupid, silly and childish." If we do that all the time — playing the Parent role — we've brought the wrong tapes to the party. The Child in us is important, then. As Adults, we should still be able to get down on our knees and play games with children.

As the true and untrue statements of our parents were duly recorded on our Parent tape, so our Child tape records the fearful as well as the joyful events mentioned above. Children well remember the times they were compared unfavorably with their brothers and sisters. They may even have made some of the comparisons themselves. "Why aren't you a good athlete, like Joe?" "Why can't you make good grades like Jean?" "Why can't I be like my Dad?" And the tape will continue to run even in our adult years — until we turn it off ourselves.

The proper use of TA will help us to do just that. We can censor these "taped instructions" that have been running our lives. Like a seasoned quarterback who calls his own plays, we will no longer have to wait for signals. Of course, we still follow the prearranged game plan plotted out by ourselves and the coaches (using what we know to be good and true from our Parent tape); but now we are free to change the plays to fit the reality of the situation. We are beginning to see the light. A good friend, a good counselor, or a nice quiet talk with a brother or sister about how mom and dad raised them and us can be one of the most enlightening moments of life. Suddenly, we become Adults.

Scripts as Models

Shakespeare said it best: "All the world's a stage. . . ." Somewhere between the ages of three and seven, we were handed our part, given our lines, and told to go out there and play our part in life. Mary's parents told her that she was very smart and that she would be famous some day. Frank, on the other hand, was told — or he overheard it said — that he was not smart.

This may be one of the best explanations why difficult people are difficult. Perhaps they are just playing their part. They are only living up to somebody else's expectations. Every play has a hero or heroine, and the supporting cast always has a villain. Since, in their estimation, they are incapable of heroic actions, the part of villain is a natural for them. And they play it to the hilt.

Another reason why some people are difficult is because they found out early in life that by being obnoxious others noticed them. Their feelings of inferiority have caused them to withdraw into themselves and thus receive little *positive strok-*

ing. They then opt for *negative stroking* which is the only way they can receive recognition. (See *I'm OK — You're OK* by Thomas A. Harris, M.D., page 69.) We open the stage curtain because we hope to receive applause when it closes. This type of difficult person opens it to get "booed." And though this form of recognition is not what most people seek, it does prove to others that he/she — the obnoxious one — does exist.

Does all this mean that people are robots, that they are not free, that they are simply following a script or listening to taped instructions from their brains? Eric Berne and other TA people would say, "No. It might sound like that, but people actually choose the ego states they use or avoid."

However, many people are not *aware* of their *decision*, especially if they tend to play their Child or Parent tapes most of the time, and refuse to use ANALYSIS on their everyday behavior. If certain people are unhappy and don't know why, TA offers help. The solution to their problem will be found in the tapes or the scripts they are following. Those who feel the need may either join a TA group, or study some of the books on the subject listed on page 127 in this book. TA will wake up the Adult in them and make them more *aware* of the games they are playing and all the subtle ways they try to get *strokes*. Then they will be able to make a *decision* (in TA it is called a Redecision) to follow a new script. As Adults, each one can say, "Now that I have my head on straight, this is how I want to act with so-and-so the next time I meet him or her." From that moment on, they turn off the old tapes and stop using the old scripts.

TA asks people to develop the Adult in themselves, to turn off their prejudicial Parent tape in their dealings with themselves and others, and to allow the happy Child in themselves to take the center of the stage. Eric Berne describes the secret of happiness as "the ability to say three words, 'Yes, No, and Wow!' " The "Yes" and the "No" constitute our Adult decision-making power. The "Wow" expresses the happy Child who wakes up each day amazed at the gift of another day. But Berne also warns against the use of the words "But" and "If only." These are the words of the hurt Child, the loser, the difficult person. "If only I was like my brother . . . If only I had gone to college . . . But what happens if I go out on that stage and nobody likes my acting? But what if I call a play as quarterback, and the play doesn't work — or what's worse, suppose I fumble?"

The theory of the TA program is magnificent. But, like all theories, it takes hard work to put it into practice. For example, a 58-year-old mother of several married children would not find it easy to play the Adult and the Child with those same children. We don't call mom, "Rita." We call mom, "Mom." Can we expect mothers, fathers, mother superiors, governors, presidents, generals, or a TV actor who has played the same role for ten years to start playing different roles immediately? Can we expect a person who treats us like a Parent and expects us to treat him or her like a Child change overnight and take on the role of Adult? And what about the People of God? For centuries they have been told what to do, what was right, and what was wrong — both in confession and in homilies. Can they learn overnight the sound moral principles so necessary for the development of a healthy Adult conscience? The Adult in all of us says, "This seems to be an unreasonable expectation," but it also says, "It is more than reasonable to start trying."

SUMMARY

In this chapter, we have considered two specific ways of understanding ourselves and others: imitation of models and the use of transactional analysis.

We often act and react to others with a model in mind. When people don't live up to our model for them, we usually label them as "difficult persons." Becoming aware of the models we use is helpful. Becoming aware that there are other models than the ones we use and know is often even more helpful.

We have also described Transactional Analysis, a theory about our behavior as human beings. Within us are three ego states, or inner selves, that we can play in any given situation: the Parent, the Adult, or the Child. All three ego states form the pattern of our lives, but our Adult role should be in control. The purpose of TA is to describe what is happening between ourselves and others (our transactions), and to teach us how to analyze the situation with a view to improvement. Shakespeare would call it holding "the mirror up to nature." We look in the mirror and become more aware of ourselves. And the end result is improvement of our relationships.

6
DIFFERENT FOLKS, DIFFERENT STROKES

Perhaps one of the reasons why we find people difficult is simply because they are different. Some like it hot; some like it cold. Some people like the window open; some like it closed. And even then no problem exists unless we *have* to be in the same enclosure with them.

For centuries, people have tried to find out why this is so. And, although no one likes to be labeled, numerous categories have been invented. We hear such remarks as,

"He's a typical German (Irishman, Italian, Frenchman, etc.)."

"She's a typical nun (schoolteacher, housewife, etc.)."

"They are typical southerners (northerners, easterners, westerners)."

"What else could you expect from a teenager?"

Despite the fact that every person *is* unique, we continue to classify, label, and put people into slots.

Lady Burton, wife of Sir Richard Burton (English explorer and writer), wrote that there are four sorts of people:

He who knows not, and knows not he knows not:
  he is a fool — shun him.

He who knows not and knows he knows not:
   he is simple — teach him.
He who knows and knows not he knows:
   he is asleep — wake him.
He who knows and knows he knows:
   he is wise — follow him.

Max Lerner, the newspaper columnist, once said that there are two types of people: (1) those who tended to close circles and shut people out, and (2) those who open circles and get involved with others.

George Seferis, poet and former Greek diplomat compared people to "the hunters and the hunted."

Loren Eisely, the scientist and writer, maintains that there are only the "tough and the tender-hearted."

Most of us are familiar with the classical division of people into four temperaments (the choleric, sanguinic, melancholic, or phlegmatic). And we accept our everyday classifications because they are useful and constructive. We are given a name, a social security number, a title. And these make voting, drinking, working, collecting taxes or blood, and many other human actions and interactions that much easier. But there is also a kind of labeling that can be destructive. "Don't hire her, she's a 'weirdo,' or she's a Black, or she's a woman, or she's a divorcee." Labels like these anger us. They can prevent us from getting to know and read the other person.

All the above personality types — and many others not mentioned here — should help us to understand that difference does not necessarily spell difficult. Here we will describe in more detail several other popular classifications. Our purpose is to aid the reader in his or her understanding of other people — especially those considered "problems." Our classifications are divided *according to outlook, according to needs,* and *according to functions.*

OUTLOOK PEOPLE

We are all familiar with the words "optimist" and "pessimist." Looking at a glass partially filled with water, the optimist says it is half-full, and the pessimist says it is half-empty. Most of us have heard these verses:

Two men looked out prison bars;
One saw mud, the other stars.

Pamela always looks at the sad side of life. Walter ruins almost every happy conversation by bringing up the latest tragedy.

Were Pamela and Walter brought up by gloomy parents? Were they extremely deprived as children? Pessimistic parents might be a cause; but there are many cheerful people whose parents were chronic complainers. And Helen Keller fought her multiple handicaps with an inspiring optimism.

We are not really sure just why optimists are optimists and pessimists are pessimists. But there is no doubt that both types of persons exist in our world. To find out what you are, here is a little quiz:

- Do you tend to see the bright or the dark side of things?
- How would your best friend or worst enemy describe your attitudes?
- Do you enjoy the scenery along the way even when you're lost?
- Do you cause happiness *wher*ever you go or *when*ever you leave?

NEEDS PEOPLE

Another way of classifying personalities is according to their needs. What are people looking for? Knowing their values system, their needs, gives us an understanding why they act the way they do.

Being – Having

In his novel, *A Young Couple*, Jean-Louis Curtis tells the story of a marriage that began to break up immediately after the honeymoon. Giles and Veronique possessed opposing personalities. He was the type of person who wanted to BE. He was happy being alive, contemplating life as it happened to him, always seeking inner harmony. Veronique, on the other hand, was the type who wanted to HAVE, to POSSESS things. She dreamed of having a life full of luxuries, leisure, and pleasure. Their differing needs form the theme of the novel.

Power – Achievement – Love

Professor David McClelland, a behavioral psychologist, categorizes people according to certain inner forces: the need for power, the need for achievement, and the need for love in personal relationships. Some people's greatest need is to have power — to have an impact on others, to be recognized, to be important. But other people are achievers. They want to get the job done and then find newer worlds to conquer. Still others are different. Love is their main driving force. They get their greatest joy and satisfaction from personal relationships and will sacrifice other satisfactions to reach that end.

Inclusion – Control – Affection

William Schutz, a therapist, author of *Joy* and *Here Comes Everybody*, moves in a similar vein. He writes that we all bring three needs, INCLUSION, CONTROL and AFFECTION, into our dealings with other people.

To exemplify these needs, let's take the meeting of a parish council. It will help us to understand people much better if we turn the spotlight on the thirteen persons who are present. They are there to consider what the parish ought to do for the youth of the parish.

Three people in the group have AFFECTION as their main need and concern. They wanted to be members of the parish council because they saw it as a chance to make good friends. Their principal need, then, is to establish close emotional ties with people — one to one. When they walk into a meeting, they give their close friends a warm hello and perhaps a big hug. And during the meeting, they may possibly be more concerned about the feelings of close friends than about the issue of improving parish programs for the youth of the parish.

Six people belong to the parish council because of their high need for INCLUSION. They see it as a way to become known, to become prominent. They need to know that people know they are members of the council. Jack and Harry, both of whom are known as "jokesters," see the meeting as a ready-made audience. Nancy always needs to have her name mentioned in the published minutes of the meetings. The other three have much the same needs.

The final four members are concerned about getting something done. They are more interested in CONTROL than in being known or accepted. Dominance rather than prominence (the need of persons concerned with INCLUSION) is their forte. If the meeting bogs down in an argument among these four people who have CONTROL as their principal concern, we will see four people whose main interest is to win or at least be on the side of the winner. However, the persons who seek INCLUSION would rather be losing participants than winning non-participants. And those concerned with AFFECTION will grow nervous during the argument because what is being said may hurt their relationships with some of the members of the council.

If people see themselves in any of the above ways, expecting everyone else to be like they are, the entire group has a problem. As described above, they are more interested in themselves than any possible program for the youth of the parish. Until they see this for themselves — and do something about it — they will remain very difficult people to handle.

FUNCTIONS PEOPLE

Carl G. Jung, the great Swiss psychoanalyst, spent many years of his life trying to figure out why people have difficulty understanding each other. His *Psychological Types,* published by Princeton University Press, proposed the theory that the people of the world are divided into *introverts* and *extroverts.* Later, he postulated four functions and eight types of people. Here is a short description of his findings.

Introverts and Extroverts

According to Jung, people are born either introvert or extrovert. We are all familiar with these words; they convey the idea of opposites. It is said that opposites attract. According to Jung — and most married partners agree — people marry their opposites. A man may find a woman fascinating not only physically but also psychologically. She's different. This can lead to great possibilities but also to great misunderstandings. If it does not lead to growth, trouble brews.

Picture a marriage in which the husband, Joe, is eighty percent an introvert and only twenty percent an extrovert. His wife, Mary, is the direct opposite. She belongs to the Altar Rosary Society, goes bowling, does volunteer work at the local hospital, and is always involved in outside activities. Joe, who is very quiet, loves to watch sports on TV; and he doesn't need company to enjoy the games. He also loves to read. For years, Joe and Mary have learned to accept their differences — with only an occasional disagreement.

But when Joe retired, he told Mary what he had been planning all those years of married life. His dream was to fix up their small house in the country and live his retirement there. They moved. Eight months later, Mary went into a severe depression. She couldn't stand the quiet of the country. She wanted to be with people.

Are you an introvert or an extrovert? Which of these two basic patterns do you follow? Answer the following questions to find out for yourself.

1. Yes ___ No ___ If you have to give an answer to someone, would you rather write that person a letter than pick up the phone and talk to that person directly?

2. Yes ___ No ___ Do you go to the store with only a vague idea of what you want — knowing that the salesperson will help you figure out what you want when you get there?

3. Yes ___ No ___ Or when you go shopping, do you generally have a clear picture of what you are going to buy so that the people at the store will not attempt to sell you something that you don't have in mind?

4. Yes ___ No ___ Do you usually show or display your immediate reactions to questions or things that happen?

5. Yes ___ No ___ When someone asks you a question, instead of coming right out with an answer, do you usually like to take a few moments to reflect about your answer?

6. Yes ___ No ___ Or do you usually answer questions aloud so as to find out what you think about the question asked?

7. Yes ___ No ___ If you go to a party, are you usually one of the first who wants to leave, so as to get home for some peace and quiet?

8. Yes ___ No ___ Do you find it easy to talk, greet, and be with strangers? For example, do you greet people in an elevator or in the parking lot coming out of church?

9. Yes ___ No ___ Or are you usually quiet and reserved when you meet new people?

10. Yes ___ No ___ Do you find it important to recognize and be recognized by others?

11. Yes ___ No ___ At a party, do you find yourself listening with one other person over in a corner, rather than talking with a big crowd of people in the center of the party?

12. Yes ___ No ___ At a party, do you enjoy lots of people, games, action, and, if it's a good party, tend to be one of the last ones to leave?

13. Yes ___ No ___ Are you more of an introvert than an extrovert?

14. Yes ___ No ___ Are you more of an extrovert than an introvert?

15. Yes ___ No ___ Would you rather answer questions like this with pencil and paper than answer them vocally in front of others?

Extroverts tend to answer the even-numbered questions "Yes" and the odd-numbered questions "No." Introverts tend to answer the odd-numbered questions "Yes" and the even-numbered questions "No."

Jung pointed out that neither of these types is better than the other. He believed that we are born with both of these fundamental approaches to life, but that one predominates. Of course, some people are extreme introverts or extreme extroverts. Their task in life is to strive for a more judicious mixture. And in our dealings with others, we should learn to understand our opposites.

Four Functions

Jung soon noticed, however, that not all introverts act alike and not all extroverts act alike. There seemed to be limitless variations in human individuality. So he devised the theory of the four functions: Thinking, Feeling, Sensation, and Intuition. Here is the graph he used to show how people function as individuals.

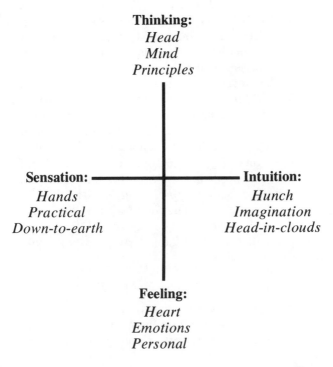

Thinking:
Head
Mind
Principles

Sensation: ——————— **Intuition:**
Hands   *Hunch*
Practical   *Imagination*
Down-to-earth   *Head-in-clouds*

Feeling:
Heart
Emotions
Personal

Some people lead with their heads, while others lead with their hearts. Some people are doers, while others are dreamers. There they are: head, heart, hands, and hunch. We notice this in the words they use in conversation:

> "I think . . . ."
> "I feel . . . ."
> "I sense . . . ."
> "I guess . . . ."

Ordinarily, we have *one* of these four functions developed more fully than the other three. This is our *superior function*. We identify intuitive-type people as "dreamers." Practical people we designate as "handy." Emotional-type people we call "feelers." Unemotional-type people, who keep "cool heads" even in a tight situation, we refer to as "thinkers."

The opposite of our *superior function* is our *inferior function*. "Hard head, cold heart" would be one example of this. But we also have our second strongest suit. For instance, we can be intuitive and feeling or intuitive and thinking at the same time. But we cannot be down-to-earth and have our heads in the sky at the same time. Nor can we be set on *enforcing the law* (the thinking type) and at the same time *feel strongly for the person* to whom it is to be applied (the feeling person). Perhaps the following pages will make this more clear.

The Dreamers and the Doers

Some people are great for dreaming up ideas, but often they are off on another dream before the ideas become realities. Other people may not dream too much, but once an idea has been born they are anxious to make it a reality.

People who are strong for getting things done are called *sensate* types. They are down-to-earth; their heads are not in the clouds. They tend to be neat. They are realists. What they see, hear, taste, touch, and smell is the basis of their knowledge. They see life through their senses. They are more apt to be doctors, mechanics, bookkeepers. Liking established routine, they are usually on time. A trip to Hawaii finds their suitcases packed weeks ahead of time. Their Christmas cards are never late. They usually have everything in place. Every home and every organization should have people — whether introverts or extroverts — who function this way. Otherwise when there is a picnic, there will be no mustard, forks, or napkins.

The *intuitive* types, the dreamers, are the ones who forget the mustard. They are the last-minute men and women of our race. They can become very difficult people for their opposites — the doers. With lots of irons in the fire, they sometimes forget that they put them there, or worse — they forget to light the fire. We wouldn't want an extreme intuitive type operating on us or keeping our books. Because their imagination is always working overtime, each word in a conversation triggers off a multitude of ideas. They are great for making suggestions, hoping that someone else will follow up on them. They tend to be the artists, the writers, the creative people, the ones who dream up new products and new fashions. Intuitive types are not afraid to ask questions. Often they are prophets.

All of us have both these gifts or functions within us. We are realists or romanticists. In some people one function will dominate the other. Others will have one function or the other to an extreme. Still others may have the two perfectly balanced. Each of us, then, has to work at developing our weaker side. The doer must dream; the dreamer must do.

- Are you a dreamer or a doer?
- Is the person you are having trouble with just your opposite?

The Head and the Heart

Our other two functions are the gifts of *thinking* and *feeling*. Some people think more with their heads, some people think more with their hearts. Some people feel with their minds, some people feel with their hearts.

Thinkers like to examine why things are the way they are. They live according to principles. They tend to be our lawyers, architects, researchers, teachers, philosophers. They are logical and analytical. Lawyers, for example, have to deal with principles of the law. If a crime has been committed, the criminal has a right to legal representation and fair trial. Feeling-type persons might find this very difficult. Their hearts would go out to the person on trial, and perhaps justice would not be done.

Feeling-type people are just the opposite of thinkers. They tend to be more aware of those who surround them. In their hearts they know when something is wrong; they can *feel* it. They like to be liked. They want harmony, peace, and no undue tension in their lives. Just as every organization needs thinking-type people who proceed with the business at hand, so every organization needs feeling-types who bring harmony and warmth with them. Coffee and doughnuts or a "happy hour" with plenty of time for small talk can be just as important for the group as the planning sessions at the big table.

- Do you think with your head or with your heart?
- Do you feel with your mind or with your heart?
- Are you concerned only with the law, regardless of circumstances?
- Are you sensitive to people and their needs?
- Do you expect a thinking-type priest to use warm examples and stories about people in his sermons?

Eight Types

People, according to Jung's theory, are first of all either introverts or extroverts. And each person — whether introvert or extrovert — exhibits the four functions of thinking, feeling, sensation, and intuition. That gives us eight types of people.

It should be understood, however, that this basic theory does not take away personality and individuality. It tells us only how people — Marie, Louie, and Angie — function. And, in doing so, it provides us with a way to understand them better. They still have their backgrounds, their experiences, their own unique selves. Moreover, they continue to develop and grow. In fact, they will surprise us at times by manifesting their *inferior* functions in preference to their *superior* functions.

There are also numerous combinations and different degrees of these various traits. Two persons may be introverts, but one may be very quiet, while the other may be talkative — but not enough to be an extrovert. Or two persons may be extreme extroverts, but one may be a sensate type with feeling as the inferior function, while the other may be a feeling type with intuition or sensation as the inferior function.

Our task, therefore, is to develop our inferior functions. *Thinkers* must learn to get in better touch with their feelings. They have to avoid being "heartless." *Feeling-type persons* must learn to use logic and reason, and not rely so much on their emotions. They must learn to overcome their tendency to manipulate thinking types. *Sensate types* must bring more variety and imagination into their lives. *Intuitive types* must learn to be more aware of time and resolve not to keep people waiting. Their objective should be to finish the important projects they have started. In general, introverted types should develop themselves by coming out of their caves, and extroverted types should begin to reflect and meditate within themselves.

SUMMARY

In this chapter we have described various ways of classifying people according to their personalities. Our purpose has not been to stereotype people, but to help us understand them. By seeing them as different rather than as difficult, we solve many of our problems.

7
ENTER, JESUS CHRIST

Many people try to improve their dealings with difficult people by using the natural means described in the preceding chapters. If they are unsuccessful at flight or fight, they talk to a third party. And, if the problem calls for it, they visit a professional counselor like a psychiatrist. They examine their expectations of others and try to deal with them. And they study personalities for the same reason. But not enough people make use of the supernatural means their religion provides to combat this problem.

To many of us, religion is a separate part of life. We go to church on Sundays and attend funerals and weddings and First Communions; but these are limited engagements only, and they seem to have little impact on our lives.

Television, sports, the dollar, work, clothes, friends, marriage, children, cars, the telephone, organizations, travel, dancing, music, sex, reading, jogging, eating, drinking, sleeping — these are our basic concerns. So often our models for living are chosen from personalities we see on television or read about in newspapers and magazines. Christ has become just some vague figure of the past.

But somewhere along the road of life the reality of God, the reality of Christ, the reality of the Spirit had better become part of our story. Only then will we become humble enough to let the rest of our illusions crumble all around us. "For everyone who exalts himself shall be humbled while he who humbles himself shall be exalted" (Lk 18:14). And like Paul, Augustine, Francis Thompson, we can say from the ground — from our darkness — to the Presence in every crisis, "Who are you?" And the voice will answer,

I am Jesus, the one you are persecuting (Acts 9:5).

I am the one who can give your restless heart rest (Augustine).

I am "The Hound of Heaven" from whom you seek to escape (Francis Thompson).

RECOGNITION

What knocks us to the ground might be a gentle breeze (a sermon, an early morning walk along the ocean, a remark by a friend) or a mighty wind sweeping across the waters (a sudden death, a heart attack, a family crisis, the end of an affair, the loss of a job, an unexpected failure). Any one of these may turn out to be the most important moment in our lives because at that precise instant we become *aware* that we must make a life *decision*.

For the searching Augustine, that moment came in a garden when he heard these words being chanted over and over again: "Take up and read. Take up and read." And so he picked up the Bible and read the first words that he saw: "Let us live honorably as in daylight; not in carousing and drunkenness, not in sexual excess and lust, not in quarreling and jealousy. Rather, put on the Lord Jesus Christ and make no provision for the desires of the flesh" (Rom 13:13-14). And he tells us in his

Confessions that immediately a peaceful light streamed into his heart and all the dark shadows of doubt fled away (*Confessions,* Book 8, 29).

When Paul, Augustine, and Francis Thompson found themselves at rock bottom, it was then that they found God. For some alcoholics the time comes when they, too, find themselves at rock bottom. And this is the moment when they embrace a Higher Power who helps them decide it is time to rise and walk in a new direction.

And it will come to all of us who have listening hearts. We all must pass through our "dark night of the soul." And if our hearts are listening, we will wake up to the rhythm of our lives. Are we ready to make a decision?

YOUR CHOICE

"What do you think of the Christ?" (Mt 22:42)

The reality of Christ — the Presence of Christ — has become meaningless to many people. He has been spoken of in so many churches, in so many sermons. Have you become numb to Christ? Is he asleep in your memory?

God, our Father, had a dream. He willed Jesus Christ to become a major factor in the flow of each person's life. "The Word became flesh and made his dwelling among us" (Jn 1:14). The love of the Father flows through the Son to all people.

Jesus used the constant dynamic of *awareness* and *decision* to spread his message of love. His parables, healings, sayings, death, and Resurrection were all meant to make people really see and understand the meaning of life. They themselves were expected to make the decision to change their hearts.

- Are you aware of Christ?
- Have you taken him for your model?
- Is it one of your reasonable expectations that you can imitate him?
- Do you ask him in prayer for power and strength to understand yourself and all the people in your life?

Suppose he were to appear in person in your hometown. You peek out your window and see him coming down the street. Even at a distance he makes a deep impression on your imagination, your thoughts, your feelings.

But you refuse to receive him into your home. "How can he help me solve my problems, especially my main one that concerns my attitudes toward difficult people?" You make regular visits to a psychiatrist. You have made a study of personality types, and you know all about transactional analysis. He has nothing to offer you. So, you move away from the window. You close your eyes, your life, until you are sure he has passed on by.

With the shades drawn, you stand there alone in the darkness. You clench your fists, your nerves on edge. You are not sure whether your emotion is fear or anger. But you know that you should never have looked out that window in the Light.

You can't put it out. The Light is now shining in your darkness. And you know that your darkness will never be able to overcome it. (See John 1:5.)

Decision.

Suddenly you find yourself heading for the door. You *have* to listen to this man. You will follow him, but you will stay in the shadows. You will hear him out, but that does not mean that you will accept everything he has to say.

JESUS SPEAKS

On the street, you notice that many other people have also left their homes. You find yourself part of a vast crowd on the mountainside just outside of town. Jesus is speaking, but you're not listening. Nothing seems to be reaching you. But then he says something that strikes you: "Love your enemies!" Is he crazy? How can you turn the other cheek to Nancy or Hank? That's impossible. You calm down. But on second thought, you see his point. Those who are nice to the people who are nice to them haven't much to brag about.

Deep down you begin to realize that he's right. Whenever you avoid people you can't stand, you don't change anything. They don't change, and you certainly don't change. Jesus is asking you to be a peacemaker. He is asking you to change your heart. He is asking you to let his light shine in you. He wants you to be a model, a city set on a mountain like this one, so that all can see in the darkness. And then in the next breath he tells you not to do it to show off. The man's a poet. He is making you think. Never before have you heard a sermon like this.

You sit there in the shadows, off to the side — in your darkness — thinking over and over again his words, "Love your enemies!" His words have the effect of a two-edged sword. They cut away at your attitudes about some of the people in your life. And in doing so they reveal the basis of Christianity — love for God and all his creatures.

Then he comes to the end of his sermon. He says that there are two kinds of people in life: the wise man who builds his house on rock and the fool who builds his house on sandy ground.

He leaves you spellbound as he walks away with his disciples. You and the entire crowd begin the journey home. Most of you are quiet. You need time to reflect all this light.

JESUS HEALS

Sometime later you hear that Jesus is in a certain house. You take time off to find out just what he has to say. Once more there is a great crowd. And a strange thing happens: Some men begin to lower a paralyzed man through the roof right down in front of Jesus.

You smile at the bizarre scene; but then the entire crowd grows silent, wondering what Jesus will do. And Jesus surprises you. He tells the man his sins are forgiven. Imagine that. The Pharisees turn red in rage. They are there only because he is Number One on their list of difficult people. They object to everything he does. He just can't do anything right.

But Jesus reads their minds as well as their clenched fists and angry eyes. He says, "Why do you harbor these thoughts?" (Lk 5:22)

Instead of waiting for an answer he turns to the paralyzed man and heals him. He tells him to stand up. And the man stands up. Jesus can heal both the inner and outer man.

The crowd is paralyzed in amazement. But it is the paralyzed man who breaks the trance. He begins to dance with joy and to praise God in a loud voice. And the crowd begins clapping their hands and rejoicing — all of them, except the Pharisees.

You stand there watching the Pharisees. You actually feel sorry for them — until you remember Jesus' words to look into your own eye first. You start walking home thinking about the whole incident. One word, one image, really strikes you. It is that sentence Jesus tossed to the Pharisees: "Why do you harbor these thoughts?"

You remind yourself of the many thoughts of resentment toward others you have harbored for so many years. And you see that you are just like the Pharisees.

JESUS RETURNS

Now, despite your self-accusations — perhaps because of them — you continue to seek him out and listen to his words. Then one day he approaches you and says, "Today, I'm coming to your house."

And Jesus comes. You have a great meal together. Jesus eats with a sinner. Then at the end of the meal, almost casually, he asks, "By the way, where does that door lead to?" You turn red in the face and stand up, saying, "What door?" He answers, "The one you're now standing in front of." And you say, "Oh, this is just the door to the cellar. You don't want to go down there. And besides, it's very dirty." But Jesus answers, "No problem. Let's go down and look around. I'm used to cellars. You never know what you'll find in them."

So you both go down to the cellar. At first Jesus just looks around, saying nothing. But then he starts asking questions, lots of questions. "What are these pictures over here along the wall?'' You blush, ''Well, Jesus, those are pictures of people who are always on my mind. I can't stand them; they bother me. But, Jesus, I promise you, I'll try to forgive them.'' Jesus answers with an ''Oh?'' Then with his finger he writes in the dust on every picture the numbers ''70 x 7.'' You ask him what that means. He smiles and says, ''Oh, that's the number of times you will have to forgive them; that is, if you want to have inner peace. And these darts here on the table — you'll have to throw them at something else.''

Silence. You both stand there quietly for a long time. Then Jesus says, ''OK, where is it?'' And with forced calmness you reply, ''Where is what?'' And he answers, ''You know. The book!'' You say, ''What book?'' He continues to look you in the eye and smile. You have no other choice: ''All right, it's over here.''

You keep it hidden in the bottom drawer of an old desk. Unlike most of the other stuff in your cellar, the book has no dust on it — a sure sign of how often you have used it. And when you hand it to Jesus you feel an enormous weight leaving your shoulders.

Mystified, you have to ask him, ''Jesus, how did you know I had it down here?'' In answer, he says, ''Those who harbor resentments usually keep their private collection of hurts written down carefully somewhere in the cellar of their hearts. And as soon as someone says the wrong thing or pushes the wrong button, out it comes. They can quote chapter and verse, word for word, what the other person said or did, sometimes even 20 or 30 years before.''

Then Jesus says, "By the way, if you wish, I can take this off your hands. I'll get rid of it for you. And I'll also take your other book — the one you haven't shown me yet."

You begin to weep. He comes over and gives you an embrace. You can't believe that he is going to take your other book too. Taking a deep breath, you pull yourself together and go over to remove the book from that same bottom drawer. You always keep it underneath your collection of hurts. You hand it to him and look him deep in the eye, saying, "Thank you! Thank you for coming!"

With that, you head back up the stairs for the dining room. You feel light-headed, free, alive, a new person. He takes a last sip of your wine and a piece of your bread as he heads for the door. In his hands are your two books. You are glad to get rid of them. Maybe next week you'll want them back, but right now you are happy that they are gone.

At the door you exchange good-byes. You stand there watching him. He turns, smiles, and waves good-bye again, saying, "Hope to see you again soon."

You walk back into the house after he disappears from view. Because this experience has been so new to you, you are unable to describe your feelings. The living room is filled with light. Your cellar door is open. All is quiet, yet "Silent Music" fills your heart. Jesus has come to your house. Jesus has come to take away not only your book of hurts and resentments but also the book that listed all the major sins of your life — all those sins you had confessed so many times but were

never able to forgive yourself for having committed.

• What do you think of the Christ?

SUMMARY

This chapter has asked the all-important question, "What do you think of the Christ?"

Jesus Christ enters all the dynamics of life.
Recognition of this fact must happen before
conversion can take place.

You can have a conversion experience. Sometimes Jesus invites himself; sometimes you have
to invite him. Your choice rests on whether you
hear Jesus speak and whether you accept his
healing.

8
STARTING WITH OURSELVES

Jesus does not leave us empty. He gives us a choice and clearly describes both roads (the narrow and the wide) and both houses (the one built on rock and the one built on sand). When we are ready to be emptied even further, he gives us some new words to replace our old ones. He hands us a new book to replace the books he took away. He gives us a new vision, with new scripts, new tapes.

Jesus' words can help us. He knows how we feel. We can build our house on them, stone by stone, saying by saying, parable by parable, book by book — Matthew, Mark, Luke, and John.

But we need time to listen to his words, to be aware of them, to study them, to wrestle with them, and to pray over them. And above all we need time to compare them with our present philosophy, our present assumptions, models, theories, expectations, and ideas about life and how to deal with the people in it.

Once we receive the full impact of his words, we feel the need to make a decision about our lives. If we see that Jesus' way is better than ours, are we prepared to walk in that new way or not? It seems so barren and cold. We feel like Francis Thompson and Saint Augustine who feared that if they accepted Jesus, they would have nothing else. But Jesus warns us: ''How narrow is the gate that leads to life, how rough the road, and how few there are who find it'' (Mt 7:14).

OUR PRESENT MOTIVATIONS

What motivates us at the present moment in our lives? What are our sources of inspiration? If they are only newspapers, magazines, books, records, and tapes, there is something lacking. Words of human wisdom are helpful, but we need words of divine wisdom in this instance.

- What are your goals?
- What makes you tick?
- Why do you really do what you do each day?
- Why do you treat certain people the way you do?

Religious Inspiration

Many people receive motivation and inspiration from their religion. Yet there are some people who say they have no religion. They don't go to church anymore. It doesn't seem relevant to them. Charlie says, ''I don't go to church anymore because all I hear about is 'money, money,money.' '' And people don't go near Charlie. They say, ''We avoid Charlie because all he ever talks about is preachers who talk about 'money, money, money.' '' Martha gave up her religion because she felt that the preacher seemed out of touch with reality. She now says that she no longer has a religion.

But in reality everybody has a religion. We wrap our lives around something, or someone, or some ideal.

Every day we listen to sermons — our own inner monologues. We keep telling ourselves what we should be doing.

We all go to church every day. We have our own inner temple — our sacred space — where we worship our god, or gods, or God.

Biblical Inspiration

Many people receive their motivation and inspiration from the Bible, but there are some who do not accept the Bible. They label it as being "out of touch." It was written for another time and another culture, not for modern men and women.

Yet we all have a bible within us. Our bible is a collection of prayers, songs, stories, laws, proverbs, history, legends, insights that have become a part of our outlook on life. Obviously we don't call it a "bible," but that's what it is. It contains our ideas on who God is and what he wants of us.

Often our bible is not the word of God, but the word of man. And, unlike the inspirations of the Bible, the words can be misleading. For example, some people seriously believe that "material success is an index of how much God loves a person." Some would also believe that, "the higher the income, the better the person."

These beliefs are not written down on paper. They are assumptions on which we base our everyday lives. They are opinions about money, people, marriage, family, anger, love, forgiveness, strangers, work, and how to deal with difficult people. Some of these beliefs are strong and some are weak, but they form the substance of our bible.

Are we aware that all these inner beliefs run our lives? Carved on our inner walls, like graffiti, are sayings and slogans like these:

- "Take care of number one."
- "Count to ten before you scream."
- "In this country, anybody can make it to the top."
- "A rational approach to problems is better than an emotional approach."
- "Do to others what you would have them do to you."
- "Everybody cheats."
- "Don't feel guilty."
- "The end justifies the means."
- "Give people a second chance, but if they burn you the second time, get rid of them."
- "God's will be done."
- "If the marriage doesn't work, get a divorce."
- "I'll never amount to anything."
- "Forgive and forget."
- "If you do cheat, don't get caught."
- "Everybody has a price."
- "If it doesn't hurt anybody, it's ok."
- "Everybody is basically selfish."
- "Nobody else ever had a problem like mine."
- "Money runs everything."
- "I never do anything right."
- "God can solve your problem if you turn to him."

Moreover, there are personal experiences, stories, memories, impressions that we never even put into words, although they play a pivotal role in our lives. These, too, help form the content of our unwritten bible.

Do we ever examine our "bible" thoroughly? One way to make us more aware of these things is to keep a diary, attend a retreat or a marriage encounter, or read a book like *Integrating Values,* by Louis Savary, S.J.

We can also achieve deeper awareness with the aid of psychiatrists, psychologists, or marriage counselors. For example, Ann has been fed up with 23 years of marriage to a "sports addict." Bob has season tickets to the local pro basketball, football, and baseball teams. If the games are on TV, nobody in the house is allowed to watch anything else. Why is Bob the way he is? Is he aware of his behavior? For answers to these questions, Ann goes to a professional counselor. Her reason: She and the children have lost the man of the house. Ann hopes that she can find help for herself and Bob.

If both Ann and Bob receive counseling together, they will begin to see that their attitudes toward sports arises from their separate backgrounds. Ann has detested sports from childhood. Bob has always loved them. Bob has shown a lack of maturity on the one hand; but Ann has shown a lack of tolerance on the other. In any case, the difficulty has arisen because of the value systems employed by the two individuals.

Obviously, the gospel according to Mom, Dad, Neighborhood, and Television has plenty of impact on our lives. Newspapers, magazines, words spoken at school, at work, at the tavern — all these become the sources of our inspiration and, at times, desperation. Even the songs we sing have a deep influence on our conduct. Some are rich in thought; some are the insane ramblings of people "spaced out" on drugs.

Are we fully *aware* of who we really are? Do we actually know what motivates us in our actions? Are we willing to improve our outlook on life? If so, then we must make a *decision*. We must decide to compare our unwritten bible values with the written Bible values inspired by God.

INSIGHTS OF JESUS

Years ago Bruce Barton wrote a book about Jesus. He called it *The Man Nobody Knows*. Unfortunately, what the title says still stands. We usually picture Jesus in the glory of his divinity. Do we do this to avoid the call to imitate his humanity?

The Gospels paint a beautiful picture of the humanity of Jesus. He watched the birds of the air and admired the lilies of the field. He stopped to observe the fishermen pulling in their nets, and a farmer sowing seed in his field. He associated with the blind, the lame, the lepers, the deaf, the widows, and the Pharisees. He was grateful for camels, swine, sheep, and goats. He inspected trees and saw that by their fruit a tree is known. He loved children and knew the weight of millstones. He noticed that some people liked to get the places of honor at table. He listened to and thought about the sermons and the parables told by the rabbis. He watched how people spent the Sabbath. He noticed wide roads and narrow doors. He watched the rich, the poor, the tax collectors, and especially the eyes of people. He read the signs of the times. He learned lessons from everyone and everything — barns, beggars, and birds.

But he often abandoned the external world for the inner world. He went into the desert, the mountains, the garden for one purpose — to pray. The content of his prayer became the message he preached. And that is why he "progressed steadily in wisdom and age and grace before God and men" (Lk 2:52).

So one day he came out of the water, out of the desert and walked into his own synagogue. Standing up to do the reading, he was handed the words of the prophet Isaiah. "He unrolled the scroll and found the passage where it was written:

'The spirit of the Lord is upon me;
    therefore he has anointed me.
He has sent me to bring glad tidings
    to the poor, to proclaim liberty to captives,

Recovery of sight to the blind
    and release to prisoners,
To announce a year of favor from the
    Lord' "
(Lk 4:17-19).

Then he told all the people assembled that this Scripture passage was now fulfilled in their hearing.

And Jesus walked out of that synagogue a rabbi — a teacher — a giver of insights. He gave light to the world, sight to the blind. He let his light shine before all.

How do we deal with the difficult people in our lives? We look to Jesus for insights. Insight improves outlook. We listen to his words; and, like Mary, the mother of Jesus, we treasure all these words and reflect on them in our hearts (Lk 2:19; 2:51).

THE WAY OF JESUS

The kingdom of God is within. This is where we start. This is where the seed roots itself — quietly below the surface (see Mk 4:26-29).

To deal with difficult people we must first make ourselves less difficult persons. The way to do so is pointed out by Saint Paul in 1 Corinthians 13:1-13. We need:

> understanding,
> wisdom,
> prayer,
> compassion,
> honesty,
> kindness,
> patience,
> constancy,
> forgiveness,
> and trust.

These qualities make it easier for us to love God with our whole being and to love our neighbor as ourselves. But Jesus taught us not only *how* to deal with people we find difficult but also *why* we should treat them with love. He shows us the way.

Happiness comes from doing God's will. Unfortunately, however, these words about "God's will" often go unnoticed. We have heard them too many times and have become immune to them. They are like the rug on the floor — always there but rarely noticed.

Specifically, God's will for us is "that all may be one" (Jn 17:21). As the three persons of the Blessed Trinity are one (see Jn 14:26) because they are united in love, so we are to become one because we are united in love for God and for others.

On this divine level, of course, we cannot know God as God. But we can know his plan and can affirm him in many ways (as Father, Shepherd, Rock, Mighty Fortress). And though our analogies are imperfect, they do give us an insight, a glimpse into God which can become a source of great inspiration to us.

On the human level, we all recognize that we feel something special, something transcendent, something God-like when we are united with one another — in marriage, in family, in a parish, in a crisis. If we sense God's presence and mystery in autumn-falling leaves, in snow-capped mountains, sunrises on the ocean, then holiday family gatherings, weddings, get-togethers should give us an even more personal dimension of unity. In some way when we are united with each other, we sense God's presence. "Where two or three are gathered in my name, there am I in their midst" (Mt 18:20).

A friendship, a marriage, a family, a parish, a convent, a rectory, a city, a country, a world should all give glimpses of God. This is the dream of Jesus "that all may be one as you, Father, are in me, and I in you" (Jn 17:21). And when people are like God — knowing and loving each other — they mirror God. Sharing food and thought together, exchanging humor, renewing friendships — these are signs of loving unity. They are clear evidence that we all need the meeting of an I (me) with a Thou (you) for survival. The writer of the Book of Genesis and many modern authors have pointed this out directly and indirectly.

Love Activates God's Plan

"God is love, and he who abides in love abides in God and God in him" (1 Jn 4:16). Jesus repeated this insight time after time. The Good Samaritan exhibited this God-abiding love; he forgot racial and legal differences and took care of the man who was mugged (see Lk 10:30-37). In the story of the rich man and Lazarus, the rich man failed to love; he did not even acknowledge the existence of Lazarus (see Lk 16:19-31). Two men went up to the temple to pray. Both prayed, but one had love only for himself. He had "I" trouble (Lk 18:9-14).

Our journey to God rests on relationships. We learn to love from our parents. Then by example we learn to love one another. When we discover what love is, we discover God. Saint John, in one of the best letters we can ever receive, tells us this clearly: "If anyone says, 'My love is fixed on God,' yet hates his brother, he is a liar. One who has no love for the brother he has seen cannot love the God he has not seen"(1 Jn 4:20).

Humanly speaking, the best moments of life are those when we love and care for others. They are the moments when we forget all about ourselves. Those sleepless nights taking care of a baby with colic, or helping a neighbor with a flooded basement, or visiting an aunt in a nursing home, or

taking the time out to play with a lonely child —
these are examples of unselfish love. Jesus gave
us this insight centuries ago. He went about doing
good: healing, helping, feeding, touching, urging,
arguing, saving people. "This is my command-
ment: love one another as I have loved you"
(Jn 15:12).

The early Christian Church learned this lesson
well. People noticed that Christians loved one
another (see Acts 2:44-47). Today, we, the People
of God, are called to this same love.

Lack of Love Spoils God's Plan

Unfortunately, however, not everyone abides
by this insight of Jesus. And that is why there are
so many difficult people in the world. Jesus chided
the Pharisees and scribes for their lack of
awareness of those around them and their lack of
awareness of the inner life. They were concerned
only with externals. Jesus told them that this was
all wrong. What was on the inside — their attitude
and approach to life — must be their main
concern. "Wicked designs come from the deep
recesses of the heart: acts of fornication, theft,
murder, adulterous conduct, greed, malicious-
ness, deceit, sensuality, envy, blasphemy, arro-
gance, an obtuse spirit. All these come from
within and render a man impure" (Mk 7:21-23).

As we saw in chapter one, it is sin that is at the
heart of the difficulties we have with people.
Briefly put, sin is evidence that we lack love. This
was the insight of Jesus. And this will be our
insight, too, if we delve into the crevices of our
hearts. When we pray to the Father in private, he

will show us what we need to know about ourselves (see Mt 6:6). He will help us to decide about changing our lives.

CONVERSION

Many commercials on television and in the news media show us people before and after they try a new product. Conversion from being a difficult person to a loving one is something like that. Out attempts at following God's original plan for our lives will usually mean a new edition or at least a revised version.

The same dynamic is at the heart of Alcoholics Anonymous and weight-watching programs. Such persons need to see themselves sober or thin before they can change. When they "hit bottom" or "break the scales," they begin to crave a new image, a new vision.

Many old timers will remember the poster of an overweight person with this caption beneath it: Inside every fat person there is a thin person crying to get out. Well, Christ's message is somewhat similar: Inside every person there is a better person (more patient, more understanding, more loving) dying to get out.

That idea of crying and dying to get out is a necessary process in conversion. And because conversion is a lonely experience we need help from a friend (a counselor), as we saw in chapter two. We can also profit from models, as described in chapter three. If television models can convince us to fast for the sake of our bodies, then Jesus and the saints can convince us to fast for the sake of our souls.

This, of course, cannot be done overnight. We have to slow down and take time to pray over the changes we are determined to make. To ease the way, perhaps we could join a Christian community where we can be at home in our new way of living. In company with others we will learn to die to the "old" and put on the "new." "If a man wishes to come after me, he must deny his very self, take up his cross, and begin to follow in my footsteps" (Mt 16:24).

How Do Conversions Happen?

Often we think of a conversion as taking place at one specific point in time. We picture Saint Paul falling to the ground and into the arms of Jesus on the road to Damascus, or Saint Augustine hearing a voice from heaven urging him to read the Letter to the Romans — events that completely changed their lives. But usually conversions are preceded by a series of experiments and failures. The dramatic breakthrough comes only after trying and trying again. Even the conversion stories based on seeming coincidence — like walking into the wrong church or happening to sit down next to the right person at a party or on a plane — began long before in the depths of the heart.

Jesus once gave a powerful description of the psychology of conversion and why some conversions last and some do not. He said there were four types of people who hear the word of God. Some are hard like a well-traveled road. The word never penetrates. They are as ungiving as concrete. The surface is what is important to them; others control their lives. Secondly, there are some who are shallow. They receive the word joyfully; but, because they have little depth, they do not give it a chance to grow. They are like people who buy books because they look good or because a title sounds interesting, but they never get past page 5. Thirdly, there are those who are counter productive. The message reaches them, but they have too many other seeds planted in their lives. Anxieties about life, desire for wealth and power, and cravings of all sorts choke off the deeply planted word. And lastly, there are those who are productive: They hear the word and because it becomes firmly rooted and is cared for, it produces thirty, sixty, and a hundredfold. (See Mk 4:2-20.)

Is It Possible to Change?

In this area of conversion, there are two kinds of people: those who believe people can change and those who think they cannot. Which side we are on depends on our attitudes toward ourselves and toward others. Can we change?

The story of Nicodemus in the New Testament answers the question we are posing here. He came to Jesus in the dark to find out if Jesus was the Light. Jesus turned the conversation back to Nicodemus — to get him to look in on his inner life. He wanted Nicodemus to start thinking about the possibilities of the kingdom within himself. He wanted him to think about change. He told him that he must be reborn. (See Jn 3:1-21.)

As we read this story, we can identify with Nicodemus. We approach Christ on our own terms — in the dark — lest our friends see us. And like Nicodemus we often fail to understand what Jesus is saying. Nicodemus seemed unaware of the inner world. Birth meant birth. A womb was a womb. "How can a man be born again, once he is old? Can he return to his mother's womb and be born again?" (Jn 3:4)

This is what conversion and change is all about. We need to become like little children once again. Change means starting life all over again. It means that we take a good look at our value systems, our religion, our outlook on life learned from mom, dad, relatives, and friends. It means that we go back into the womb — back to the Lord who created us. But to do all this demands taking time out to discover what the Father wants of us — to discover why he created us in the beginning.

Follow Nicodemus

To the Pharisees Jesus was a difficult person. How did they deal with him? Their actions constitute a lesson on how *not* to act. They talked behind his back. They tried to trap him. They were blind to his virtues and deaf to his message. They refused to change. So in the end their only solution was to have him condemned to death — a frank admission that they could not deal with him.

But Nicodemus was the exception. He was a Pharisee who broke from the crowd. He came to Jesus with questions, confessing his ignorance. Like the other Pharisees, he seemed to take things literally and failed to understand what goes on below the surface. Yet he had the courage to try to understand Jesus and what he was teaching.

Nicodemus changed, and the Gospels seem to indicate that his conversion lasted. When Jesus came to Jerusalem for the Feast of Booths, the crowds went wild. This infuriated the chief priests and the Pharisees. They sent the temple guard to arrest Jesus, but they could not because of the crowd. In the back room debate that followed, Nicodemus spoke up in defense of Jesus: "Since when does our law condemn any man without first hearing him and knowing the facts?" (Jn 7:51) This was a courageous challenge to the others because Nicodemus knew where they stood. So they taunted him: "Do not tell us you are a Galilean too?" (Jn 7:52) Later, Nicodemus was present for the burial of Jesus.

We too can change. But, as Nicodemus was told by Jesus, we must be reborn. We must rid ourselves of false attitudes and open ourselves to the way of Jesus. With love as the basis of all our actions, there will be one less difficult person to deal with in the world. And because we ourselves are loving, we will find it much easier to deal with difficult people.

SUMMARY

In this chapter we have seen that the way to deal with difficult people is to start by dealing with ourselves. The first step is to become aware of and to make a decision about the sources of inspiration which motivate our lives. The second step is to become aware of the insights of Jesus — that his is a Way of love. The third step is to make a decision for conversion. We *can* change, and conversion will make it easier for us to deal with difficult people.

9
IMPORTANCE OF DIALOGUE

Are you familiar with the TV commercial showing an auto mechanic pointing out that you can pay him now for a small part or pay him later for major repairs? He stands there, a philosopher in overalls, saying, "Pay me now or pay me later."

If we learn how to face calmly our difficulties and misunderstandings with other people, we can avoid bigger problems in the future.

We tend to avoid minor repairs in our relationships. Then suddenly a major breakdown occurs. Shouting matches, separate bedrooms, divorces are the usual results. Since we did not talk to the other person in small matters, we find it next to impossible to discuss big problems with him or her.

We saw in our last chapter that conversion is an excellent way to solve our problems in this area. But even after such a drastic change in ourselves we still have to contend with the other party. And this is why dialogue is so important and necessary.

We see compelling reasons for this on all sides. The daily news tells us about wars, revolutions, uprisings, and power moves by special interest groups to acquire even more power or money. Scaled down, the same pattern happens in every office, home, group, and relationship. Only after flight or fight proves unworkable do people finally see the need for "peace talks." Both sides need to die to themselves, to make concessions and sacrifices, to listen to each other.

This chapter is about dialogue — the what, when, where, and how of it. It will show how dialogue is a necessary part of the spiritual development of the followers of Jesus. We all participate in the Paschal Mystery. There can be no Easter Sunday without a Good Friday. The seed must die before it can burst forth into life. No cross, no crown. No pain, no gain.

Dialogue is for everyone. There are no exceptions. Jesus erased all boundaries, all limitations, and all divisions. We cannot come into this world except through a mother and a father. We all need each other. The people in the boiler room must speak with the people on the bridge. Those in the cockpit must keep in contact with those in the control tower.

WHAT IT IS

What is the meaning of dialogue? It is the careful clarification of assumptions between people.

Just as we all have expectations, so we all make and have assumptions about many things. We assume things about: God, the Russians, the Bible, wrestling, how to cook pot roast, and how our neighbors should take care of their children, their lawn, and their dog.

We often assume that our difficult people are selfish. They are purposely doing what we do not like. We assume that they are avoiding us because of something we said eleven years ago at a Fourth of July family picnic.

Dialogue makes use of words, but they are not its main concern. It touches on the models, meanings, values, attitudes, expectations, and assumptions that are below the surface of words and actions. Through it we come to know and understand other people.

Some of us deliberately avoid dialogue because it may eliminate our favorite pastimes. We may find out that we have been wrong about these people for so many years. If we sit down *with* them — getting to know them — we may no longer be able to talk *about* them.

Michael Korda, who has written books and articles on how to be successful and powerful in the business world, advises people who want to have an advantage over another person not to look the other person in the eye. Dialogue, however, has an entirely different purpose. It demands an eyeball-to-eyeball approach. It is Adult to Adult — not Parent to Child — conversation for the sake of clarifying (discovering and explaining) the meanings behind people and their words and actions.

So often, however, we are like tape recorders. We have certain assumptions about a wife, a husband, or a fellow worker. We recorded them years ago, and we have been playing that same song about them in our heads ever since. Sometimes we turn the volume up and let another person hear our assumptions, but most of the time we keep the volume down and play it over and over again in our hearts.

The word "careful" in our definition of dialogue means that we proceed *with care*. Dialogue does not consist of opening a complaint box and saying to the other, "Here, read these." No, it means that two people sit down to clear the air about feelings, assumptions, and complaints. It deals with personality differences, limitations, expectations, sin, etc. Because of this, dialogue is an absolute necessity in our lives.

Married people need to dialogue. The second day of marriage is different from the first. People change, and change can be growth or decay. A couple can move from enchantment to disenchantment — from Fantasy Island to Devil's Island. As somebody once put it:

> The glances over cocktails
> that seemed so sweet,
> don't seem so sweet
> over shredded wheat.

Dialogue is a must for people who have to deal with each other on a regular basis. If we have wrong assumptions about somebody with whom we work, we should clear the air; otherwise, our work will suffer.

If we care enough to live our very best and are willing to take the risks involved, then dialogue can and will be a means to better relationships with difficult people.

WHEN TO DIALOGUE

When is the best time for dialogue? Our answer depends very much on the trust level of the people involved. How high is it?

Earning the right to really level with another person usually requires time. Look how long it took to get the Vietnam peace talks moving. The participants argued about trivial things at first — like the shape of the peace table. Look how long it has taken Catholics and Protestants to come together for ecumenical dialogue. Look how long it takes to negotiate labor disputes.

If it took years for the walls of assumptions, expectations, complaints, and anger to pile up, then it may take as long to tear them down. So, we will use the Golden Rule — "Do unto others . . ." — to judge the right time. We will ask ourselves: "When would be the best time for someone to approach us?"

This first step is the hardest. Proud parents clap when baby Joe takes his first step, even if he falls. The first step in dialogue is to go to the difficult person and say, "May I talk to you? Are you busy?" or "Hey, we have to do some talking about this. When is the best time for you?" Sometimes quick decisive statements like these will open the door for an appointment with the other person. Sometimes, too, the door will be slammed shut.

Yet it is a start. It makes the other person start to think. It makes him or her aware that we exist. Then we try again.

WHERE TO DIALOGUE

Where is the best place for dialogue? Obviously, this will depend upon the person concerned and the problem involved.

Sometimes a car is the best place for talking. A father may want to talk to his son who is "goofing off'' too much. Perhaps for years the two have been charting different courses, sailing on different seas. He asks his son to help him pick up some two-by-fours at the lumberyard. He figures that while driving along their small talk will clear the way for big talk. Talking in a car gives a person who is scared permission to avoid having to look in the other's eye. Another advantage is that the other person is a captive audience. Perhaps, after a great breakthrough between the two of them, they can drop into a McDonald's or a Burger King for a hamburger and a shake. This may very well be the best father-son banquet ever.

In marriage problems, atmosphere also plays an important role. Some couples have the practice of taking a weekend off and heading for a motel to really thrash out their problems. Motel rooms and baby-sitters cost money, but they are cheaper than divorces. Such a weekend may lead to the decision to seek a third party for marriage counseling. Then, too, it may end up in disaster, but it is an honest attempt to change the direction of a marriage that is on a collision course. Some ships pass each other silently in the night. Other ships crash because they become lost in the silent fog of non-communication.

Once two people decide when and where to dialogue, they expand their opportunities for communicating with each other.

HOW TO DIALOGUE

How do we dialogue? Like the answer to the question on how to handle a porcupine, our answer is: "Very carefully."

Seriously, however, here are seven steps to keep in mind if we really want to begin to communicate or dialogue with someone we find difficult.

1 Prepare an Agenda

On becoming aware that we are having difficulty with a particular person too often, we take pencil and paper in hand. We jot down remarks, situations, incidents, and as many of the specific details as possible — everything that bothers us about this person. It is amazing how many problems will dissolve on parchment paper. But if this is a really difficult person, one or two items will still remain.

2 Decide to Talk

On the advice of a third party we decide that the problem has to be faced. We cannot keep on avoiding or fighting this person. We have to live with, work with, or deal with him or her on a regular basis. So we make a decision to talk with the other party.

3 Make an Appointment

We go to the person at the best time and place and invite him or her to a conversation. "What's the best time the two of us can talk about something that's bothering me?" We set up an appointment. This is not easy, of course, because we will be actually talking to the difficult person and not about him or her. Till now, our resentments have been aired only in our heads or to a third party.

4 Proceed Slowly

At our meeting we slowly unfold some of the details about what's "bugging" us. We don't dive right in; we test the waters. We watch for body language indicated by the other person's eyes, hands, face, throat. We view him or her as an Adult, not as a Parent or a Child. We can do these things because we have rehearsed and planned the situation beforehand. However, this does not give us the right to take advantage of the other person's weaker position. If we are "unfair" in any way, dialogue will not take place. At all costs, we must avoid flooding him or her with the hitherto pent-up waters of our resentment. So we move slowly, remembering that in the People Zone we proceed at 15 miles per hour.

5 Explain the Problem

No dialogue can proceed unless the problem is brought out in the open. We reveal our assumptions, our expectations, how we see the problem. We do not pass judgment. We have not walked in the other person's shoes. No, we tell him or her who we are and how we really feel. This helps the other party to understand what's going on inside our skin, inside our shoes. And maybe, if we are proceeding prudently, the other person will begin to reveal who he or she really is.

6 Specify Clearly

If we feel or assume that our problem stems from lack of attention or failure to show love on the part of the other person, we don't just say, "I don't think you love me anymore." We would proceed in the following way. Martha (whose problem is jealousy) says to her husband: "When you spent at least two hours at the party with Jane, I really got uptight; and I'm not sure, but it looks like I still have my old problem with jealousy. Can you help me?"

7 *Listen Attentively*

Throughout our dialogue, of course, we have been listening. We pay close attention to see how the other person sees the situation. We keep checking and rechecking, trying to understand the other's viewpoint. We repeat what the other party is saying, to make sure that we are hearing correctly.

At first the other person may not realize what is happening. (People who are out of touch with others are probably out of touch with themselves. They are surprised to hear that what they did or said was offensive to others.) We talk as an Adult to an Adult. We make sure that we do not give the impression that this is a "win-lose" situation.

We treat the other person with kindness and love. By asking him or her to sit down at our table to share our bread and our thoughts, we show that we see the other person as an equal. And as equals we want to solve our problems together.

WHAT TO DO IF DIALOGUE FAILS

If dialogue fails, what do we do? We search for the reasons. Perhaps we were at fault. Maybe we ourselves forgot the important word — "careful" — in the definition of dialogue. *How* we say things can make all the difference in the world. Or it could be that the other person was hampered by pride, fear, or some other human fault. People resist change in their lives.

Then, what do we do? We learn from Jesus. He wanted harmony, but he did not want peace at any cost. He rocked the boat when this became necessary. Ask the Pharisees whom he confronted. Ask the money changers who were driven out of the temple. So, too, a parent, a wife, a husband, an engaged person, a nun, a priest, a teacher, a boss — each one may very well have to take similar steps in a difficult situation. Then, it is hoped, the other person will return to the bargaining table.

In the Gospel of Matthew, Jesus tells us how to deal with someone who won't dialogue with us: "If your brother should commit some wrong against you, go and point out his fault, but keep it between the two of you. If he listens to you, you have won your brother over. If he does not listen, summon another, so that every case may stand on the word of two or three witnesses. If he ignores them, refer it to the church. If he ignores even the church, then treat him as you would a Gentile or a tax collector" (Mt 18:15-18).

These words do not sound like the gentle Jesus speaking. He preached that we should love our enemies. But they are doubly interesting, because Matthew was a tax collector and Jesus treated him with care. And, although they seem to ignore the principles of modern communication theory, they boldly face the facts of the situation.

What Jesus is saying is that if we really care about persons who happen to be difficult, we go to them privately at first. We dialogue, if possible.

But if that does not work, and they really need help — because they are disrupting a home, a convent, a parish, an office, a relationship — then we bring in others if that is the kind of shock therapy needed. And if banishment will help to wake them up, we use that strategy too. (Of course, we remain in touch, even while showing disapproval of their actions.) And our motive throughout is always love.

Jesus came here on earth to wake us up with the warmth of his love. He abhors homes where each room is an isolation ward. Silent, frigid partners are not part of his plan for happy marriages. Tension-filled factories and scandal-full offices belie every word that he preached. No, he calls people to a love of God which will proclaim itself in love of neighbor.

Because of the weakness of our human nature, we will always find dialogue necessary in our lives. Difficult people need to know that we care enough to reach out to them. If they are wounded and hurt as a result of experiences beyond our grasp, then they are no different from the man lying on the road between Jerusalem and Jericho. We must be good Samaritans and care for them. Read that story in Lk 10:25-37 once again. We cannot walk by a difficult person.

SUMMARY

Dialogue is the careful clarification of assumptions between people. It means that we find out what makes us tick first of all. Then we begin to clear the air with the other person.

Dialogue is not a shotgun blast. That is a sure way to kill it. If, in the early stages, we fail to make progress, we keep trying. We continue to clarify what is going on between ourselves and the other person.

We pick out the best time, place, and circumstances to discuss the problem with the other person. We show that we care enough to try to heal any and all wounds.

However, if the other refuses and it seems we cannot heal the rift, we either call in other people — if that seems necessary — or we withdraw and wait for a better day. The motive behind all our methods is love.

10
FROM THE TOP
OF THE MOUNTAIN

Most of us are looking for a magic solution to all our problems on how to deal with the difficult people in our lives. Books can help. They can give us a better understanding of ourselves and others, show us how to proceed, and motivate us to act. But books do not change people. Only people can change themselves.

St. Francis of Assisi knew this, when he prayed:

Lord,
make me an instrument of your peace.
Where there is hatred, let me sow love.
Where there is injury, pardon,
where there is doubt, faith,
where there is despair, hope,
where there is darkness, light,
and where there is sadness, joy.
Divine Master,
grant that I may not so much seek
to be consoled, as to console,
to be understood, as to understand,
to be loved, as to love.
For it is in giving
that we receive.
It is in pardoning,
that we are pardoned.
And it is in dying,
that we are born to eternal life.

This one prayer is a well-organized program or "platform" on how to deal with people. Books come and books go, but this one prayer has an appeal that will last forever.

Does it work?

It works if we follow it faithfully. In fact, it can be a "Declaration of Independence" for us if we really learn to answer hate with love, injury with pardon, doubt with faith, darkness with light, and sadness with joy. It can set us free from anyone who disturbs our peace. We are in charge of ourselves. We decide whether we are to be instruments of peace or instruments of war.

In chapters 7 and 8 of this book, we saw that conversion or change is not just something external. It takes place when we let the Lord come right into our hearts. Conversion is a one-to-one experience, a one-to-one conversation, a dialogue between the Lord and ourselves.

Sometimes we concentrate so hard on changing difficult people that we forget we ourselves must change before any success can be had. Only in this way can we become instruments of the Lord's peace.

VIEW FROM ABOVE

Did you ever stop to look out over your town, your city, from a mountain, a hill, or some high vantage point?

Let's suppose that you have. It is a beautiful autumn afternoon and the leaves have started to change. There below lies your world.

Thoughts About Others

At first, everyone looks so small — except Betty and Joe, two of your difficult people. They stand out "like sore thumbs." You stand there thinking.

You begin to talk to yourself. "Yes, that's why Betty is so difficult. She's a sore thumb. Maybe she's hurting and needs attention and healing. Maybe that's why she bothers everybody at work. This must be her way of getting attention. She must have tried other ways and never got noticed. It worked with her parents and teachers; and now she has all the people at work sitting up and taking notice."

From this distance you begin to realize that Betty's mannerisms have nothing to do with you. She really doesn't even notice you. She is just speaking *at* you to say things *to* herself. When she belittles you she is only trying to enhance her own ego. If that is true, then her real problem is that she has a poor self-image. She must feel ugly things about herself.

That must be the reason why some people don't get as upset about Betty as you do. Like beauty, then, difficulty must lie in the eye of the beholder. There are two kinds of people: those who find difficult people difficult, and those who do not. Everybody at work knows that Betty is a pain and a bother. Why, then, are you the only one who always gets uptight about her, while others don't seem to let her bother them?

Continuing to look down, you see Joe coming out of his house. He, too, sticks out "like a sore thumb." He upsets you because he has "I" trouble. His every sentence is peppered with "I. . .I. . .I. . .I. . . ." Whenever he walks into a room "heads start turning" — the other way. People say under their breath, "Oh, no, not Joe again. Well, here goes another good conversation."

Yes, Joe has "I" trouble. No matter what anyone says, he has to top it off with, "Well, I . . . ." He's the world's greatest authority on everything. Actually, he doesn't put other people down; he puts himself up.

At first glance, it appears that Joe has a different problem than Betty. He doesn't seem to have a poor self-image. But with a sudden insight, you realize that Betty and Joe *do* have the same problem. He, too, is talking out loud to himself — telling himself that he's OK. Fortunately, he doesn't belittle you; however, he isn't aware of you either. Like Betty, he has a poor self-image; he just manifests his in a different way.

These new insights about Betty and Joe make you feel at peace with yourself. You have just discovered a secret; now it will be easier for you to deal with difficult people. Whether you climb up a mountain or plunge into a desert the result should be the same; both places give you ample time to think deeply about particular people in your life.

Longfellow once said, "Believe me, every man has his secret sorrows, which the world knows not; and oftentimes we call a man cold, when he is only sad." You cannot really know what is going on inside Betty or Joe or anybody else; but now that you have "been to the mountain" you understand them better. And you also have discovered the secret of peaceful coexistence.

Thoughts About Yourself

After thinking about other problem people, your thoughts instinctively turn to yourself: "I am the one who should plan to change. The other person may not change, but I certainly can." You may not be able to dialogue with some people, but you can make some changes within yourself; you can change your attitudes toward people you find difficult. By changing yourself you change the problem.

One big change you can make is to love the sinner but hate the sin. C. S. Lewis, a very quotable English author, once said that he had heard this distinction for years, but he did not really advert to it. Then he realized that he had been following it every day of his life. So you can love others even when they do things you find unbearable. You can love a daughter who is into drugs or is living with someone without benefit of marriage and still disagree strongly with what she is doing.

You may not have enough power over your immediate reactions to certain persons, but you can control your deeper feelings. Why should you let other persons control your feelings — especially when they don't even know they are doing it? Why should you let their mannerisms bother you? Why should you let their behavior ruin the whole evening, the whole party, the whole day? They won't if you have "been to the mountain."

VIEW FROM BELOW

You continue to stand there, and now your thoughts turn once more to the people down below. But this time you ask yourself what *they* think about you. You look down and see your house, your street, your family, your neighbors, your church, your place of work. What do all those people think about you? How do they want you to change?

A breeze starts to chill the air. You head for the car. There is still time for some thinking.

You find yourself looking into the car mirror. You sit there staring at yourself. You really look yourself in the eye. A strange feeling comes over you. Never before have you looked into a mirror like this. Usually, you only glance at a mirror to see if you are presentable. But now you are looking into your very self.

Do the people down below find you difficult? Could you say to your wife (or husband): "When can we talk? I've been thinking that there's much room for improvement on my part. Is there anything about our relationship that bothers you? Here's a piece of paper, honey. Write down three things I do that frustrate you. And please make them specific. Give me the times, places, and circumstances."

For years now you have been avoiding your own eyes. You have been so busy keeping the other person's score you have lost track of your own. You have been traveling at top speed through life — always doing something, seldom pausing for anything. Why? Because if you stop, you will have to think.

In these quiet moments here on the mountain looking into the mirror — into your own eye — you begin to see that the best way to deal with difficult people is to start dealing with yourself.

VIEW THROUGH JESUS' EYES

Now you ask yourself, "Where did all these thoughts come from?" And suddenly it dawns on you that Jesus has been saying these things to you for years. But you have been too busy to listen. Jesus looked out over the people when he spoke these words:

> Why look at the speck in your brother's eye when you miss the plank in your own? How can you say to your brother, "Let me take that speck out of your eye," while all the time the plank remains in your own? You hypocrite! Remove the plank from your own eye first; then you will see clearly to take the speck from your brother's eye (Mt 7:3-5).

"That's it," you say to yourself. "I have been trying to deal with difficult people without first dealing with myself."

You begin to pray — perhaps for the first time in months — as you sit there looking down into your town. Lights start to go on one by one in the homes below. You are fascinated; you have never witnessed anything like this before.

You feel somewhat the way Jesus must have felt as he looked out over the city of Jerusalem, weeping: "If only you had known the path to peace this day; but you have completely lost it from view!" (Lk 19:42)

You are weeping too, but yours are tears of joy. You have found "the path to peace this day." Hitherto, you had "completely lost it from view," because you had focused your eyes on the wrong person.

A light goes on inside your house — your self. Jesus' *way* is the path to peace. If you go back home now and try to be an instrument of that peace, if you try to treat people the way he treated them, then you, too, can be light — his light in the world.

You look down and picture Jesus going through your town. It is filled with all kinds of people: the deaf, the blind, and the lame. You are one of them and so are the people in your life. You have been blind and deaf and halting to each other. Some are emotional cripples. Some are Pharisees — concerned only with externals. And you see Jesus dealing with each one, using that same touch, that same love, that same healing power recorded in Matthew, Mark, Luke, and John. All these years you have expected Jesus to put up with you — with your sins, your mannerisms, your moods — while you, like the unforgiving servant, have treated your brothers and sisters without compassion. (Read Mt 18:21-35.) Jesus worked miracles. People changed. You can change. You can be healed. You can work miracles too.

Darkness has set in, but there are lights everywhere. You turn the key and start the car. Slowly, you wend your way down. Gentle peace fills your soul. You have been to the mountain, and now you must return home to face the realities of life. Only you and God know what will happen next.

YOUR DECISION

Nicholas Murray Butler, president of Columbia University in the early part of this century, once said that there are three groups of people in this world:

— a small elite group who make things happen;
— a somewhat larger group who watch things happen;
— and the great multitude who don't know what happens.

Few people really know what is happening between themselves and certain people whom they label as "difficult." And those who do often only "watch." The purpose of this book has been to motivate you to join the "elite group who make things happen" in the area of dealing with difficult people.

It is hoped that you now have a greater *awareness* of the life patterns — your expectations, assumptions, models — which motivate and inspire you. And, presumably, you are now more aware of the insights of Jesus about this problem area.

It is also hoped that these pages have enticed you to make a *decision* to follow the Lord's WAY. Unless you are already a living saint, this will require on your part a conversion — a journey to the Father, with a stopover at Calvary. It is a journey through life imitating Christ by caring, dialoguing, challenging, understanding other people. And when you do this an amazing thing happens: people change — especially you. This is mystery, the Paschal Mystery: a dying and rising with Christ.

As you proceed on your journey, you will notice that you are not alone. Others, too, will be trying to increase love all over the world. At times you may become disheartened; but if you and the

Lord become partners, you will find that dealing with difficult people is not so difficult after all.

SUMMARY

This last chapter sums up the message of these pages: *awareness* and *decision*.

This book urges you to join the group of people who make things happen. Dealing with difficult people calls for love and care on your part. But it also demands that you start with yourself — your inner life. It summons you to the top of the mountain to get in touch with the Father, so that you can come down from the mountain an instrument of the Lord's peace.

BOOKS FOR FURTHER READING

The books in this list are available in inexpensive paperback editions.

Between Parent and Teenager, by Dr. Haim G. Ginott. Avon Books.

Games People Play, by Eric Berne. Ballantine Books.

I'm OK — You're OK, by Thomas A. Harris, M.D. Avon Books.

Joy, by William Schutz. Grove Press.

A Primer of Jungian Psychology, by Calvin Hall and Vernon J. Nordby. New American Library.

Unconditional Love, by John Powell, S.J. Argus Communications.

The Wounded Healer, by Henri Nouwen. Doubleday & Company.

Other helpful books
from Liguori

HANDBOOK FOR
TODAY'S CATHOLIC FAMILY
Revised Edition

Written in a direct, easy-to-read style, this book offers a great depth of understanding, hope, and help for the family unit. It includes:

- Basic ideas in Catholic theology for *today's family*
- Suggestions for Catholic family practices
- Ideas for family prayer.

Meant to foster family closeness and Catholic identity. $1.95

HOW TO DEVELOP
A BETTER SELF-IMAGE

Blends practical psychology with a Christian view of life. Discusses the person your *training* wants you to be, the person your *feelings* want you to be, and the person God *designed you to become*. $2.95

HOW TO FORGIVE YOURSELF
AND OTHERS
Steps to Reconciliation

It's sometimes hard to forgive others — but even harder to forgive yourself. This book shows how to let go of deep hurts, mend broken relationships, and learn about forgiving. $1.50

Order from your local bookstore or write to:
Liguori Publications
Box 060, Liguori, Missouri 63057-9999
*(Please add $1.00 for postage and handling for orders
under $5.00; $1.50 for orders over $5.00.)*